AN INTRO
POLITICAL

An Introduction to Political Astrology

By

CHARLES E. O. CARTER

President of the Astrological Lodge of London
Principal of the Faculty of Astrological Studies

L. N. FOWLER & CO. LTD.

1201/3 HIGH ROAD
CHADWELL HEATH
ROMFORD, ESSEX RM6 4DH

First edition 1951
Second impression 1969
Third impression 1973
Fourth impression 1980

SBN 8524 3004 3

Printed offset in Great Britain at
The Camelot Press Ltd, Southampton

CONTENTS

INDEX OF HOROSCOPES

FOREWORD

During the Second World War there was, as was natural, a considerable amount of interest in Political Astrology, and my attention, as well as that of many others, was attracted to this work as never before.

It soon became apparent that new methods and a vastly more copious and more trustworthy collection of data were needed; but this was more easily perceived than effected. Nevertheless something was achieved and now it seems worth while to place on record some of the conclusions that were reached and as many of the data as are sufficiently reliable as to merit preservation. Furthermore, it is helpful to examine difficulties even if they cannot immediately be overcome.

At the moment the horoscope of the individual, or nativity, appears to be the principal field of astrological study. But actually the nativity cannot adequately be considered as isolated from the social environment, as represented astrologically by other horoscopes of greater amplitude. Could the nativities of the victims at Hiroshima all have indicated the death and ruin that overtook them on the fateful day of August, 1945? Perhaps, and yet the horoscope of that city, could it have been studied, would surely have been helpful in judging them.

Sooner or later, I believe, "mundane" astrology will have to be replaced at the top of the astrological tree, and the more the State controls the individual, the truer this will be.

Yet not much real work has been done in this field. Alan Leo's ventures into political prognostication were feeble and unsuccessful. Sepharial had brilliant achievements to his credit, and left us valuable hints, but he did not work systematically. As a result we have very little literature on this branch of our science, at least in Britain. H. S. Green's lucid and concise manual is still well worth reading and outlines all the classical methods, but it is not very original. It was first published many years ago. I do not know of any other book, published in English during the last twenty-five years, that is entirely or even principally devoted to this department of our work.

This gap in our literature is perhaps sufficient excuse for the appearance of the present work.

CHARLES E. O. CARTER.

October, 1951.

CHAPTER ONE

THE AIMS AND SUBJECT-MATTER

THE Ancients appear to have divided Astrology roughly into three kinds : there was the Doctrine of the Nativity, which was also called Genethlialogy and was concerned with individual maps of birth and all that arises therefrom ; there was Judicial Astrology, which in modern times is usually called Horary ; and there remained a mass, rather ill-defined, that was named Mundane Astrology. This comprised, one may say, all that concerned many people, rather than a single person.

Thus under Mundane Astrology came not only the rise and fall of dynasties, and wars, but also earthquakes, droughts, epidemics, the founding and destinies of cities.

The term Mundane Astrology is still in use, but the tendency seems to be to use more precise terms to denominate its several branches, and to speak of Political Astrology, or the science as concerned with politically organised groups, Racial Astrology, or the science as concerned with blood-communities, Astro-Meteorology, Astro-Seismology, and so forth.

Between the Doctrine of the Nativity or Natal Astrology, which is concerned with the individual, and Political and Racial Astrology, we may place the study of smaller groups possessing no marked national interest or influence. Thus, one may cast the horoscope of a society or club or any similar minor association. We are not concerned with such things here, except to mention them as having their place in the astrological scheme.

Our subject here is Political Astrology, or the study in the light of Astrology of politically organised and significant communities, from groups of allied nations such as might be represented by Western Union, through the Nation, down to political parties of sufficient importance to justify study.

We shall find that this study embraces, in terms of itself, most other kinds of Astrology in greater or lesser degrees. For even a single person may assume national and even world-wide significance, and thus his nativity will, to that degree, enter the domain of Political Astrology. Horary Astrology, too, may be enlisted in our service, for maps may be cast to answer questions of political import : who will win the next election, and so on.

If we look into the past we shall have no reason to congratulate ourselves upon our achievements in this field. Modern students have for the most part devoted themselves to the study of the nativity, and mainly from a psychological angle. When we look for good work in the wider and far more intricate task of Mundane Astrology, we shall find a few lucky hits and many blunders. Even these lucky hits were usually based, not on true mundane astrology, but upon deductions from the nativities of prominent people.

Thus it was easy to see that downfall awaited William II of Germany, if only from the opposition of his Sun to Saturn, and of Hitler, who had Saturn in detriment in the 10th, squared by Venus and Mars.

There was, of course, nothing wrong in thus using Natal Astrology in the service of Mundane ; but this usage has its obvious limitations. William II and Hitler might have disappeared from the scene before the two wars with which they are respectively associated had ended ; and then any deductions as to the conclusion of hostilities that had been founded on their genitures would have been invalidated.

I shall attempt to show that the methods used by mundane astrologers have been completely inadequate. Chiefly, to judge by the almanacs, and by past issues of *Modern Astrology* they relied on lunations and solar ingresses. We shall discuss these later on. Taken by themselves, they are scarcely worth casting.

" Taken by themselves " : this phrase reveals the basic error of these students. In Mundane Astrology there is no such isolation. This is true even in regard to the doctrine of nativities, properly understood, for the individual is a member of a family, a trade or guild, a nation, and so on. But usually the data for these to be scrutinised do not exist, and we manage to make shift without them. But in mundane work many factors are involved. More indeed, often enough, for any one person to be able to comprehend in his mind. Yet the attempt must be made.

Perhaps, if one had, and knew one had, the definite trustworthy nativity of a nation, one could do pretty well with this alone, studying it radically and progressing it, as one would a natus. But ingresses and lunations, taken alone, are pitifully insufficient, as all the evidence of the past bears witness. Indeed this is obvious, for the aspects in them are identical all the world over, and only the domal characteristics are differentiated, and even these are not always very different for different capital cities. Madrid is almost on the meridian of London.

Much may be excused the ordinary mundane astrologer, for the data required for a proper study of his subject are in a state of confusion. When the late war (1939–45) broke out, the present writer, as editor of the principal astrological periodical then extant, felt called upon to make certain general predictions. But it soon became evident to him that there was very little reliable information upon which to work. As time went on, maps were examined and tested, and, in two or three years, a certain amount of firm ground had been located. Even so, the true horoscope of the U.S.S.R. had not been ascertained. Was the 1871 map of Imperial Germany still valid, or should one use either of two other maps that had been put forward by German astrologers ? What of the horoscope of the Third Reich, apparently a figure deliberately " elected " according to astrological principles ? What of the chart of the German Republic ? Should he use our 1066 map, calculated for the coronation of William the Conqueror, which unfortunately could not be progressed for lack of data, or the 1707 figure, highly esteemed by some, or that of the United Kingdom, for 1801 ? Was the alleged chart of the French Third Republic valid ? How about the U.S.A. figure ? What of Italy ?

At all events it soon became patent that lunations and ingresses, by themselves, were useless and only had importance when a planet was found exactly upon an angle—and by " exactly " an arc of not more than one degree must be understood.

There were but the nativities of King George, Hitler, Mussolini, and, later, Franklin D. Roosevelt. Also, subject to considerable question, that of Stalin. Else, all lay in doubt and had to be rejected until time and opportunity arose for a real proving.

One should perhaps add the map for the declaration of war. But such horoscopes as these are subject to the same drawback as ingresses and lunations : all aspects are the same for the country that declares war and that which accepts the declaration. Only mundane positions differ, though, as we shall see, these *may* make a very great difference indeed.

National Astrology embraces many things besides war. But in all of them the national map must remain dominant. This is the Doctrine of Subsumption: horoscopes fall into a hierarchical order, each with less field as one descends, but yet itself being the dominant horoscope of others yet lower down the scale. Ideally, at the head of all human maps, must be the horoscope of Man himself, the moment when, symbolically stated, God breathed into him the breath of life. Then would come the maps of the all-various races and nations and within these (politically speaking) those of the major parties. From another point of view, there would be those of the several great religious bodies; from yet another, the major trades and industries, and so on downwards to the individual.

We are seldom able, in practice, to consider this Law of Subsumption, for lack of data. But we could, in Natal Astrology, at least make a start by trying always to study the map of a child in conjunction with those of its parents and their marriage-map.

Be that as it may, we shall see that in mundane work the marvellous involvement of maps must be taken into consideration, at least as far as is humanly possible. Of this fact we shall offer, we trust, abundant evidence.

The aim then of Political Astrology is the study of all that pertains to the life of a politically incorporated body, or nation. It must comprehend the cultural and intellectual life, the religious life, the economic, and so forth, going through the familiar twelve-house classification (see Chapter Six).

Most will feel that to study one country alone from this extensive point of view will suffice them; and the ideal would be that there should be, in various countries, boards of members of which each member would concentrate his attention on one country, or on a small group of countries, and so the members of each board could confer and collate their opinions, and each board could, in turn, confer and collate their findings with all other boards.

It is inevitable, human nature being as it is, that one of the greatest difficulties in making scientific forecasts and judgments of other kinds is in being impartial as between one's own party or country and those that oppose these. Boards such as have been suggested above would obviate this problem. It is, especially in matters of great national importance, in a word in crises, extremely difficult for the average person to preserve a clear vision. This is aggravated by reading newspapers full of shallow and tendentious writings; and, of course, in a real emergency, an astrologer would be obliged to refrain from uttering anything calculated to give rise to "alarm and despondency," as the phrase goes.

What would have happened if an honest and clear-sighted astrologer had published an unbiased opinion of the map for the declarations of war in 1914 and 1939? Especially if he had judged them, as most did, in themselves, and had not perceived the significant correlations between them and other maps—of which matter more anon. Certainly such an astrologer would have been discouraged (gently or otherwise) from indulging in further public lucubrations.

Mundane Astrology, then, is a most intricate and difficult branch of the science; but it has its compensations. For one thing, if some of its data are in a chaotic state, others are precise, e.g., the times of ingresses, lunations, eclipses, great conjunctions and *sometimes* of political events, such as the signing of a treaty. Particulars of great catastrophes, such as fires, epidemics, and earthquakes, are recorded by scientists with all relevant detail. The same applies to birth-rates and death-rates, and to stock exchange prices and amounts of business transacted, to the prices of commodities, and to the weather. If the truth about political transactions is often hidden or distorted at the time, to shield interested parties or for other reasons, yet in the long run the facts are usually known, whereas in natal astrology the astrologer commonly hears but one side of the story, and sometimes no story at all.

Moreover, the importance and interest of great national movements and events are immense and the possible utility of true Astrology to the life of one's nation incites a patriotic astrologer to seek the way to better and better results. Further, if the restoration of public honour to Astrology be his goal, it would seem that this can be attained in no better way than by acquiring the power to foresee correctly things of national moment, with which all are concerned.

It is hoped that some of the ideas set forth in this book will encourage and assist students to labour in this particular tract of astrological soil, for it is both important and interesting; indeed it should logically take precedence over all other branches of our science, especially during the present epoch, when the life of the individual counts for so very little in comparison with that of the community, to which it is increasingly subordinated and by which it is ever more coloured.

CHAPTER TWO

THE MATERIAL EMPLOYED

Part One : *Classification of material. Astro-geology and Astro-topology. Eclipses and lunations. Great conjunctions.*

WE propose a fivefold classification.

1. Astro-geology and astro-topology are based on certain natural affinities between specific areas of the earth's surface and the astrological factors—principally the signs.

2. Various phenomena *in coelo* (to use the time-honoured term) or current phenomena that occur at or about the time of the correlated events and conditions. These may be considered in and by themselves, as we shall see, and they need not necessarily be related to other data, though it will be indicated that such correlations are in fact often highly significant. We have :

(*a*) Eclipses and ordinary lunations
(*b*) Great Conjunctions
(*c*) Stations
(*d*) Comets
(*e*) Ingresses

3. The nativities of persons of eminence : here the Doctrine of Nativities enters the field of Political Astrology.

4. Inceptionals, a term introduced by the author for the beginning, or start, of any event-series, excluding Nati-

vities, which have always had their own distinctive place, though in actual fact they are of course inceptionals.

5. The Astrology of Cycles, or world-periods.

Some of these classes may overlap. Thus from one point of view the rulership of towns and cities belongs to Astro-topology, yet horoscopes for the foundation of these may be better regarded as inceptionals, since they probably depend upon the figure for the time of their being founded. Under this head we may also place horoscopes for the outbreak of wars, for treaties, buildings of all kinds such as bridges, town halls, colleges, proclamation of new constitutions, the coming into effect of certain laws, launchings of ships, and (in Natal Astrology) such things as marriages, the signing of contracts and so forth.

We will examine these categories in some detail and will illustrate them by reference to the Great War of 1914–18 and concurrent events and conditions.

1. Astro-geology began, so far as our tradition goes, with Ptolemy, who described a highly artificial classification of the countries within or adjacent to the Roman Empire. This can have little value, and if subsequent experience has in some cases confirmed his statements, this can only be a matter of chance.

But astrologers are agreed that a clear affinity does exist between the signs and specific tracts of the earth's surface, and this is conceived as being inherent or natural and to be quite independent of the nations or races inhabiting the territories in question. However, it may be acknowledged that a race, settling in a new country, e.g., the Anglo-Saxons in New England, would probably tend to lose their racial rulership, at least in part, and assimilate to the territorial affinities of the lands they occupied.

Neither would these territorial rulerships necessarily agree with the national or political rulership, so that, in respect of a country, we ought to consider these three factors: the natural geographical rulership, the ethnological or racial, and the political.

For example, there is some reason to suppose that much of the United States is under Scorpio, for the aborigines appear to have had Scorpionic traits in a high degree. But the modern Americans exhibit predominantly Gemini qualities, whilst the map for the Declaration of Independence is considered by some as being under Gemini and by others under Libra.

Probably, however, these three factors would tend in the course of time to coalesce, and in practice it might be difficult to distinguish them.

The usual method of determining the dominant sign of a country is by the passage of heavy planets through the signs and noting the effects, if any, that are evident in the life of the nation. This, however, has this disadvantage, that the passage of a planet through *any* of the angles of a national map will probably produce marked correlates.*

The habits and cultural peculiarities of a people suggest the probable race-ruler, e.g., Cancer and the Chinese, whilst the identity of the political ruler will depend upon the setting up of the first government, modified by subsequent similar enactments. Thus the proclamation of the Chinese People's Republic appears to have taken place when Aquarius was on the ascendant, but the Chinese Republic, born in 1912, had the Moon rising in Libra.

It is suggested that when a political rulership, such as these, conflicts violently with the racial and territorial rulerships, it will be short-lived, in terms of history.

*I use this word instead of the more usual " effects " since the latter expression implies planetary causal action, which I do not accept, at least not unreservedly.

As regards these transits through signs, or ingresses as they are often styled, Uranus is a good significator, being neither too fast in motion nor too slow.

Thus Pluto touched Cancer for the first time in its present cycle in 1912 when the Republic of China came into being, and the Communist government took power soon after Uranus entered the same part of the ecliptic in 1949.

The correlates of the passage of Uranus through Gemini, as displayed in the United States, are striking: the revolution in 1776, the Civil War in 1860, and the Second Great War in 1941. U.S.A. declared war on Japan on December 8, Uranus having first entered Gemini in the preceding August.

Similarly the passage of Uranus through Aquarius, traditionally ruling Russia, brought the Revolution in that country.

We have, so far as I am aware and can conceive, no data whatever of racial rulerships, except in so far as we can speculatively deduce them from the characteristics of the races themselves. But that countries are in some sense "under" specific signs and for practical purposes may be regarded as being ruled by these, seems certain enough, however these may have arisen. But the number of countries whose rulers, in this sense, may be regarded as fairly sure is painfully small.

England is usually placed under Aries, following Ptolemy, Ireland under Taurus, Scotland under Cancer, and Wales under Gemini. France and Italy are both (!) placed under Leo. Spain is said to be under Sagittarius, Austria under Libra, Norway under Scorpio and Sweden under Aquarius, which is also said to the sign of Russia, Prussia and part of Poland! But there is much disagreement about Germany, which, like England and Denmark, is traditionally under Aries.

It can easily be perceived that such sweeping generalities can be of only very limited practical value. It is quite possible—indeed it must be—that several countries should fall under the same sign ; but unless one can differentiate in some way, little use can be made of the fact.

In any case, as we have said, not many of these attributions have been carefully examined and tested. For example, the passage of Uranus through Aquarius in the 1914–18 period assuredly coincided with appropriate conditions in Russia, Prussia and Poland—but why was Sweden exempted ? To answer this we must bring to bear other methods and ways of approach, of which Mundane Astrology has many.

Within one country different areas certainly have astrological affinities, subordinate to the common over-all rulership. In England, where several ancient races have left their stamp even unto this day in particular districts, this can be studied with advantage and much interest. The Cockney has ever been thought of as Mercurial ; the stubborn inhabitant of Sussex looks and behaves as a native of Taurus ; towards the south-west the Pisces element is noticeable—one seems, in travelling in that direction, to feel the subtle change of atmosphere after traversing the New Forest or Salisbury Plain. The north-east (the ancient Dane-law) is definitely more Martian ; the north-west (at least to the present writer) seems to have a strong Uranus value, the people being generous, outspoken, and quick to take likes and dislikes.

It is obvious that a knowledge of these " atmospheres " would be of considerable use, if they were definitely established. Still more so, information as to town- and city-rulerships : we have, however, explained above that we take these as being rather appurtenant to the doctrine of Inceptionals, since towns and cities are definitely "founded" and have inceptional maps, though very few are known, at least in a country where most of them have been inhabited for many centuries.

We give, in the Appendices, lists of the principal countries and cities of the world, in so far as anything is known about their astrological affinities, but the reader is warned that some of these, at least, are open to question.

So much, then, for Astro-geology and Astro-topology.

2. (*a*) Eclipses and ordinary lunations.

It seems likely that eclipses were, of all celestial phenomena except perhaps comets, the first that attracted man's attention. They could hardly fail to do so owing to their spectacular character, and it is scarcely to be doubted that their effect upon those early observers was one of fear. Early man regarded himself as being far more intimately involved in Nature's processes than does his modern counterpart, to whom such things "just happen" and are thought of as affecting his life only in so far as they might conceivably occasion a little temporary inconvenience, like a shower of rain. But early man did not think of such things as "just happening"; he might not, at that time, trouble to seek an astronomical explanation of the occurrence, but he would certainly look upon it as having a meaning, a message for himself and his kind. He was wont to talk (usually in prayer) to natural objects and he thought of them, in turn, as having communications to make to him. Sometimes his primitive attempts at reasoning were absurd enough, though hardly more so than many superstitious usages that may still be observed in plenty among persons who have had at least a formal education. If he put out a lamp, it was for a reason ; if then God extinguished *His* lights, it was for some reason. What was this ? How did it concern man ?

Now astrologers know that one cannot lump all eclipses together as good or as bad, in any sense of those ambiguous adjectives. But it is a fact that an eclipse of the Sun is commonly followed by disturbances that are usually undesirable, humanly speaking. Usually, too, it is the monarch or other notabilities of the country that suffer, whereas lunar eclipses more often seem to affect the common people. The same is true of comets, which must also have attracted the notice of primitive man and awakened his apprehensions, since they can be awesome objects in the clear dry atmosphere of Mesopotamia.

In modern practice it is customary to consider an eclipse (and the same principles apply to ordinary lunations) in respect of the sign in which it falls and the countries said to be in affinity with that sign according to the ideas set forth in our last section.

It should then be considered in the light of the genitures of prominent persons, especially monarchs and presidents, in order to discover its significance, if any, in that connection.

Next, a map is erected for the metropolis of the country under consideration.* Now, it is obvious that such figures have grave limitations. For they are zodiacally identical the world over. If the eclipse falls on Mars in the map, it is just as much conjunction Mars in Peru as in China : only the house-positions alter according to the latitude

*The time is a matter of doubt. In the ephemeris the time stated is that of the conjunction of the Lights in longitude, but it is open to question whether the correct moment is not that of maximum obscuration, which may differ appreciably.

and longitude of the places for which the various horoscopes are erected. In illustration of this I may refer to the map for the eclipse of August 12–22, 1588, details of which were sent me by Dr. Troinski of Berlin. The data are :

M.C.	*Asc.*	*Sun*	*Moon*	*Mercury*	*Venus*
♉ 15	♌ 27	♌ 29	♌ 29	♍ 26	♎ 11
Mars	*Jupiter*	*Saturn*	*Uranus*	*Neptune*	*Pluto*
♌ 0	♌ 28	♉ 29	♓ 15	♌ 2	♈ 10

Now the position of Sun, Moon and Jupiter almost exactly on the ascendant, even though squared by Saturn, is eminently appropriate to the mood of England at that time, just after the overthrow of the Armada. But the horoscope would not be very different if cast for Madrid ! Only the Leo satellitium would no longer have been so close to the ascendant, which would have been about $19\frac{1}{2}°$ of that sign.

It is when we compare this map with our 1066 *figure we see its special significance for England.* The critical place of Uranus, 28° 30′ Sagittarius, receives three almost exact trines from the Sun, Moon and Jupiter of the eclipse. But when we look at the natus of Philip II ("Notable Nativities" No. 548) we see how appalling this eclipse was for him and for Spain, for his Moon was in 27 Aquarius, his Mars $29\frac{1}{2}$ Scorpio, Uranus in $15\frac{1}{2}$ Gemini, and Neptune in 15 Pisces. Thus it is in relating eclipses to important nativities that their greatest value lies. Therefore I do not consider such maps of much value *in and by themselves* unless, at the place in question, a body is on an angle, say within 2°, or even less. For it is my view that *in mundane figures of all kinds house-position counts for little unless an angle is involved closely*. If an intermediate cusp (i.e., not an angle) is involved, it *may* be important, but this introduces the vexed problem of correct house-division, and this point must be left open. But, since in all these figures we have the immense advantage of an exact time and maps that are in consequence precisely accurate, they afford an excellent field for those (if such there be) who are prepared to test this matter of domification by practical means instead of pursuing it down the endless labyrinth of theoretical disputation. Verily Omar Khayyám, himself an astrologer, must have had this enigma in mind when he wrote :

> " Myself when young did eagerly frequent
> Doctor and Saint, and heard great argument
> About it and about, but evermore
> Came out by the same Door as in I went."

In 1914 there were two eclipses, one of which fell in 6 Pisces and was therefore close to Pluto (5 Pisces) in our 1801 horoscope, that of the United Kingdom, see page 27. The other, in 27° 36′ Leo, was not far from Saturn in the same map, but here the significance seems rather to be that in the horoscope of the eclipse 3½ Pisces was on the nadir at London, once again striking the note of the 1801 Pluto, a planet which was, of course, unknown to astrologers at that time. Falling in Leo, it may have had especial " effect " on Rumania, Italy and France, and its incidence on the natus of the emperor Francis Joseph was malefic. It is perhaps worth noting that on November 11, 1918, Saturn was in Leo 27° 31′. Doubtless a careful scrutiny would reveal other significances in regard to the war, but it is not our intention to make a thorough examination of the astrology of that period, but only to select examples to illustrate astrological methods.

Figure for the Coronation of William I at Westminster, on Christmas Day, at true noon, 1066

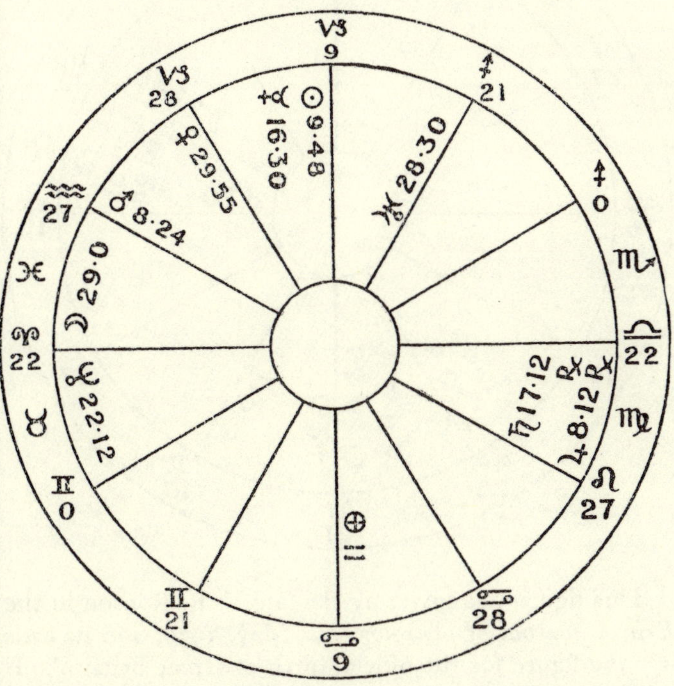

This figure appears to retain a marked significance for modern England. In particular the place of Uranus, which is in close square to the Moon, remains a highly sensitive point.

The Horoscope of the Union of England and Scotland Cast for 0 hr. 0 min. 0 sec., May 1, 1707, as at London

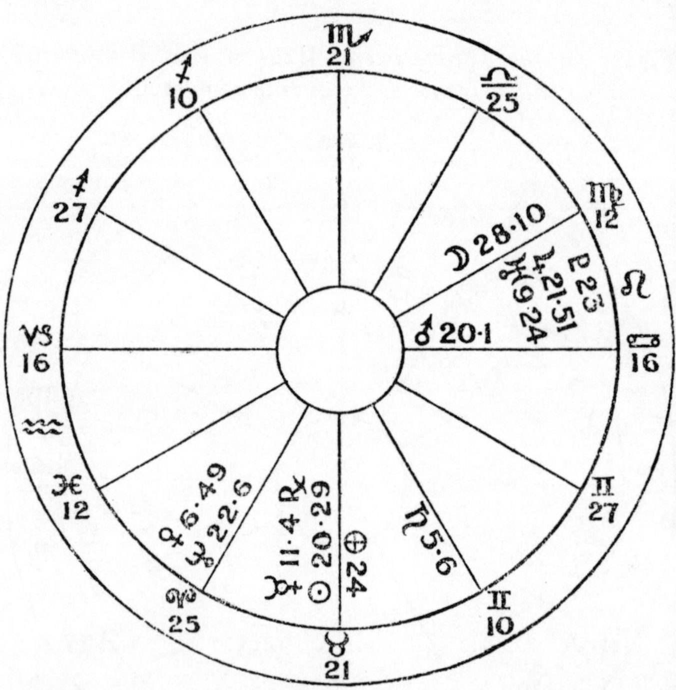

This figure was given by the late V. E. Robson in the *British Journal of Astrology* for May, 1930, and he calls it " the figure for the official birth of Great Britain." It is still worthy of some attention, but the present writer has found the 1801 map, on the next page, more reliable. But it will be seen that there are important and interesting correlations between the two, and also with the 1066 horoscope.

The Horoscope of the United Kingdom
Cast for 0 *hr.* 0 *min.* 0 *sec., January* 1, 1801, *at Greenwich*

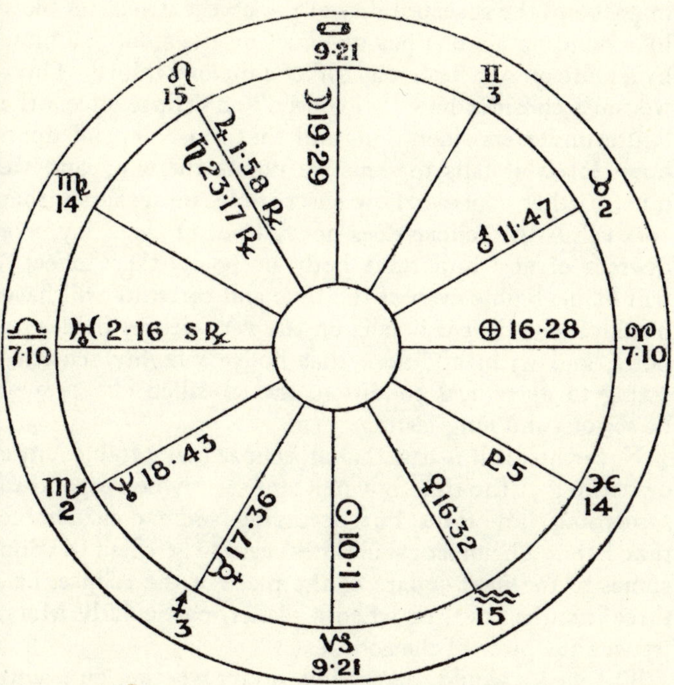

It is cast for the moment of the coming into force of the Act for the Union of Great Britain and Ireland and appears still to be a figure possessing much significance for British affairs.

A number of attempts have been made to determine how long the " effects " of eclipses endure. It is suggested that these inquiries are erroneously conceived. To reason by analogy: how long do the effects of a blow last? Clearly two factors are involved—the violence of the impact and the susceptibility of the object struck. A blow by a hand on a stone has no effect on the stone; a blow by a knife on soft flesh may inflict a lifelong injury. Thus, we must consider how "violently" an eclipse affects the figure under consideration, and that must depend upon how closely it falls to sensitive points therein; and we must further consider how susceptible, or sensitive, that spot is. If the eclipse does not fall nearer than, say, five degrees of any important body or point, the "effect" will be negligible even at the time and certainly will have no duration. But if it falls on the very degree held by a body, and if, in addition, that body is highly sensitive owing to its radical condition, the so-called effects may be serious and long-lasting.

Nevertheless it *is* true that an eclipse may produce little or nothing at the time but may apparently correspond to something important but occurring some considerable time later. The most usual times seem to be when the Sun comes to the next square of the place of the eclipse, i.e., three months later, or when a planet, particularly Mars, transits the place of the eclipse.

The writer would, personally, doubt whether an event, however appropriate in nature, could be ascribed to an eclipse that preceded it by more than a year, and he would certainly be inclined to look for some auxiliary factor, such as a direction or transit, to bear the major responsibility.

Lunar eclipses are never considered as having as long a period of valency as solars, and ordinary lunations, which in other respects must be treated exactly as eclipses, do not outlast their month.

It is only right to say that some students have given solar eclipses, in some circumstances, a valency of more than three years. But events cannot be simply correlated with any one phenomenon ; with them must be correlated not one phenomenon but a *totum coelum*, the complete pattern prevalent at that time in the life or lives in question. In this pattern certain phenomena will be outstanding, like certain markings on a carpet ; but the pattern is one integral but intricate weaving, from birth to death, one colour melting into another and one item in the design into others, each modifying or reinforcing each.

From what has been said the reader will perceive that a particular eclipse may, from the standpoint of a special mundane condition, be either of very great or very little significance.

2. (*b*) Great Conjunctions are those formed between Jupiter and Saturn, to which we may now add Uranus, Neptune and Pluto. The first two must often present a striking appearance in countries blessed with clear atmosphere, especially if they are in approximately the same latitude as well as identical longitude, and therefore are actually close together in the line of vision.

Great conjunctions are of course in the same category as eclipses and lunations, which are themselves " great conjunctions " but have received special designations.

The planetary conjunctions are thus judged in the same way as eclipses, that is, (*a*) as maps in themselves, when they are not important unless an angle is closely affected, (*b*) as affecting other important maps, and (*c*) according to the sign in which they fall.

The year 1914 affords an excellent example. There was then, on March 4, a conjunction of Jupiter and Uranus in

9° 33′ Aquarius, and it is significant that on August 4, *Uranus had retrograded to this precise position.* If we erect a map for London for this conjunction, we find the ascendant is 28° 26′ Sagittarius, only 4′ from the place of Uranus in the 1066 map, which we shall more than once have occasion to mention as a point of danger. But if the map be erected for the latitude of Berlin and 54 min. later for the longitude of that city, the M.C. is 17° Scorpio, exactly opposed to the place of Pluto in the map for Imperial Germany (see diagram on page 31). Thus, though of slight importance in itself, this figure becomes very menacing when correlated with others.

Again, Uranus in 9° 33′ Aquarius opposes the Kaiser's Saturn in 9° 01′ Leo, is conjunction Mars in our 1066 map, and opposes its own place in our 1707 chart, being only 9′ out.

One would expect Jupiter-Uranus conjunctions to bring with them revolutions of ideas rather than the revolution of anger, which might be associated with Mars-Uranus, or possibly Mars-Jupiter. Therefore it is not surprising to find this conjunction in action in the map for the Communist régime in Russia, which shows Jupiter in 9° 12′ Gemini, and in the map for the German (Weimar) Republic, of which the data are 1.30 p.m., C.E.T., November 9, 1918, Berlin, and which has Neptune in 9° 20′ Leo. The figure of the founding of the Nazi Party (6.29 p.m., G.M.T., February 24, 1920, Munich) has Neptune in 9° 30′ Leo, and that for the establishment of the Third Reich (10.30 a.m., G.M.T., January 30, 1933, Berlin) has Sun in 10° 5′ Aquarius.

Further, the map of the German Empire (which appears to be exactly correct) has 10° 0′ Aquarius on the M.C.*

*Events during the war caused me to rectify this to 9° 40′ Aquarius, even nearer to the place of the conjunction.

Map for the Proclamation of William I as German Emperor, at Versailles, at 1 p.m., L.M.T., January 18, 1871, at Versailles

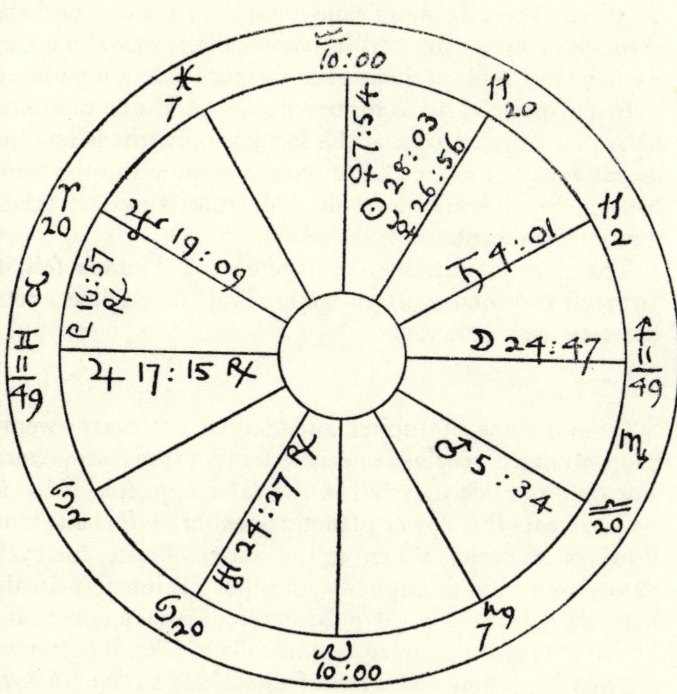

Several maps have been suggested by German astrologers as being for United Germany, such as "German Union," 6 hr. 19 min. L.M.T., December 10, 1870, Berlin, and 0 hr. 0 min., January 1, 1871, Berlin, and noon, April 16, 1871, Berlin. But the above figure appears to have demonstrated its validity throughout the two great wars.

Even if we assume that some of these may be fortuitous, it would appear that this conjunction had considerable influence on the events of the period under consideration, but it seems likely that the place in which it fell had already acquired special significance for Germany, perhaps through being on the mid-heaven of the Imperial map, as we have just said, perhaps even farther back in history.

In a map for Moscow for the moment of the conjunction 6¾ Aquarius rises, so that the locus is only just below the ascendant. Saturn is almost exactly opposed to the mid-heaven. Since Aquarius traditionally rules Russia, all this is doubly significant.

The next conjunction of Jupiter and Uranus fell in 1927–28 and then again in 1941. Thus they fall at about fourteen-year intervals.

Conjunctions of Jupiter and Saturn fall every twenty years and have received special attention from astrologers. For long periods they fall in the same triplicity, since in twenty years the slower planet passes through about two-thirds of its cycle. When, in the course of time, the cycle passes into a fresh triplicity, the first conjunction in the new element is termed a Mutation Conjunction ; and when, at very long intervals, this falls in Fire, it is termed a Great Mutation. The last of these fell in 1603 (*B.J.A.*, May, 1930) and showed the Sun and Venus just rising at London, in Sagittarius, the conjunction itself falling in 8° 20′ of the same sign.

During the nineteenth century the following conjunctions took place :

In 1802 — 4° 56′ Virgo
1821 — 24° 40′ Aries

In 1842 — 8° 56′ Capricorn
1861 — 18° 22′ Virgo
1881 — 1° 36′ Taurus

It has been suggested that these conjunctions, when falling in Earth, especially affect economic conditions and show the growing importance of this aspect of national life.

In 1901 the conjunction fell in 13° 59′ Capricorn, on November 28, and was followed after some months by the conclusion of the Boer War (Venus on cusp 9 at London). In 1921 it was in 26° 36′ Virgo with the Moon in the ill-fated area of Sagittarius (28° 36′) : the 1939 war broke out before this map had drawn to its close. Mars was close to the 1801 Saturn, and Mercury to Uranus.

Owing to the phenomenon of retrogradation, there were three successive conjunctions in 1940–41, which led to much discussion as to which was the dominant for the period.

The first (August 8, 1940) showed Venus almost precisely rising at London, which led the writer to think peace must be at hand. Actually we know that at that time Hitler made overtures which may have seemed, at least to him, generous in the circumstances. Further, during the next few months the glorious Battle of Britain defeated the Nazi plan for invasion and so, though there was no peace, there was still something like peace in Britain compared with what would have happened in the event of an invasion.

Logically one might assume that this figure would have lasted until the second conjunction (October 20, 1940) and that this would have persisted until the third (February 15, 1941).

The second figure showed a strong trine of the Moon on cusp 9 in Gemini to Mars just above the eastern horizon in Libra ; and although we must ever bear in mind that this aspect was equally present in all maps for that moment, wherever drawn, it is true that it may have applied to Britain in a special sense, since it had Mars so near the ascendant. Hence we may also see here evidence of the Battle of Britain and subsequent R.A.F. successes.

The third figure, curiously enough, again shows Moon near cusp 9, but in Libra, and trine Venus rising, so that again it might have been held to herald peace. And of course peace did come under it, but only after four years. In this figure Mars is in 28° 08′ Sagittarius !

It would be well if the priority of such figures could be established once and for all from the study of these three.

This task, however, we will not now attempt, but there does seem some reason to believe that, contrary to what might perhaps be expected, it is the first which has the distinction of being predominant. We may point out that the arc, from August 8, 1941 to " VE " Day, is 4° 45′ and that this when added to the M.C. 28° 54′ Aquarius yields 3° 39′ Pisces—in trine (to within 1′) of Venus, 3° 40′ Cancer.*

It may, however, be said that by far the most important thing that has been since 1940–41 is the explosion of the first atom-bomb, on July 16, 1945, 5.30 a.m. M.W.T. 33° N., 106° W., *and here we find Uranus on the same degree and minute as Uranus in the second map.*

Thus, as usual, it will probably be by no means easy to obtain a decisive answer to this problem.

*There are of course several suggested systems of progression for the M.C., some in longitude and some in right ascension, and so another problem arises which we cannot discuss here. In the case in point the arc is too short for much divergence to arise. It may be said though, that astrologers who wish to attack the matter of the correct progression of the mid-heaven would do well to use mundane maps of which the data are beyond suspicion, instead of human nativities in regard to which there is nearly always some degree of uncertainty.

Conjunctions of Jupiter and Neptune occur, obviously, more frequently than those between Jupiter and Saturn or Uranus.

There were three in 1919–1920 in Leo, in 1932 in Virgo, and 1945 in Libra, close to the ascendant of the 1801 horoscope.

The general value of this conjunction is inflationary, not only in an economic sense, but in the sense that hopes and fancies outsoar the normal restrictions imposed by Saturnian common sense, which condition is inevitably followed by a greater or lesser degree of disillusionment. Boom is followed by slump. Naturally this will vary according to sign, but it was plainly shown in the first of the above triad after the war of 1914–18, and again after 1945.

The effects of Jupiter-Pluto conjunctions, occurring as they do almost every twelve years, can hardly be profound, though they may act acutely at the time. There was one in Cancer in 1930, a year of devastating financial crisis, and in Leo in 1943.

There were three conjunctions of Saturn and Uranus in 1897 in Scorpio, the previous series having been at the beginning of Taurus in 1851–52. Such phenomena indicate grave stresses for the countries affected, either by their being under the sign in which the conjunction occurs, or because of its prominence in the local horoscope, cast for the time that it is exact, or in the national horoscope; and that, of course, is true of all these maps, as we have said. Thus some countries may feel them very little, and, since about forty-five years separate these conjunctions, it is clear that, except by some system of direction, it would be difficult in the extreme to follow their correlates in history. Probably, however, the "effects" would in the main follow fairly closely upon the conjunctions. Thus the 1851–52 conjunction may be thought to have had some connection with the Crimean War of 1854 and the Indian Mutiny of 1857, since both Russia and India come under Saturn and the Crimea is placed under Taurus, its ancient inhabitants having been called the Tauri.

As for the 1897 conjunction in Scorpio, there was the Transvaal War, and this country is put under Scorpio, as is Norway, which broke away from Sweden in 1905.

The last conjunction was on May 3, 1942, in 29° 20′ Taurus, close to Neptune rising in the map for the Japanese Constitution (10.30 a.m., Standard Time, Tokio, February 11, 1889). Poland and White Russia are placed under Taurus by Green and at this time the German penetration into these regions was complete. Sevastapol fell on July 1. The locus of the conjunction did not affect any of our three maps adversely, though the precedent transits of both planets to the King's radical Moon and Uranus had had devastating correlates.

There was a conjunction of Saturn and Neptune in May 1882 in 16° 30′ Taurus; and another in Leo 4° 46′ on August 1, 1917, which agrees well enough with the disastrous battles of that year on French and Italian soil. One could not expect favourable things from such a combination; it would be expected to occasion an anarchic condition, since Neptune would tend to dissolve, as it were, the bonds of Saturn. It is well known that a complete collapse of French morale very nearly ensued upon the Nivelle failure, and also in the Italian Army at Caporetto.

It is probably a coincidence, though a curious one, that both these loci fall in significant points in the maps of the two dictators, Hitler and Mussolini, who did so much to spread ruin and chaos throughout Europe. The former preceded Hitler's birth; the latter, Mussolini's rise to power. The map for Rome for the Leo conjunction shows Uranus nearly setting, and the maps both for Rome and Berlin show the Taurus conjunction near the M.C.

In the London map for the Leo conjunction the ascendant comes to the opposition of Uranus in 1926 (the General Strike) and the M.C. is in square to progressed Uranus in 1939. In 1945 Venus has almost come to the ascendant at London.

Thus it seems plain that these maps produce valid directions. Indeed the question is not so much what maps of this class are valid, as which out of several are of most practical value, since it is hardly advisable to use all, for fear of being lost in a maze.

Those that fall on an angle at a given metropolis will obviously be of importance for that country, as also those that show a strong involvement with the natus of the ruler, or of the country.

It is to be feared that the next conjunctions (1952–3) will coincide with much misery. They fall in the last decan of Libra and their stress will obviously fall in the main on Libran countries, and those having afflicted points near the loci of the conjunctions.

There was a conjunction of Saturn and Pluto on August 9, 1947, in 13° Leo, but I fear it must be left for elucidation to future writers who can see such things in perspective. Pluto is a small body and a very distant one, and often it seems to have no great value in nativities. On the other hand, it certainly seems by no means a dumb note in national astrology and during the late war its appearance on an angle, in ingresses and lunations, usually heralded an offensive by the country indicated. Its conjunction with Saturn might therefore be thought to have a paralysing effect, preventing or hindering positive action, and, so far as our own country is concerned, some might say that it denotes the paralysing of business initiative by heavy taxation and the innumerable restrictions which, wisely or unwisely, the Socialist government imposed.

On August 15, 1947, the Dominions of Pakistan and India were inaugurated and here we get a clear sign of Plutonic action—the opening of fresh chapters. Saturn, it need hardly be recalled, is the territorial ruler of India. It is suggested that this conjunction-figure may have special importance for these two countries, as well as their own inauguration-maps.

The previous conjunction was at the beginning of Cancer in 1915 and might be similarly tested in relation to China. Before that the planets met in May 1883 at the end of Taurus.

The last conjunction of Uranus and Neptune fell in Capricorn 3, in March 1821, before the latter planet was known to astronomy, and the next does not occur for 170 years. It seems difficult, to say the least, to deal with phenomena that happen so rarely, but one important point must be made. Not only do these celestial events coincide closely in time with events in the world at large, but they also reproduce their values as those born under them grow to adult manhood and take their part in national affairs. Thus, both Queen Victoria and the Prince Consort had these bodies conjoined (at the end of Sagittarius) and so the " effects " of the conjunction must have worked through them for the whole Victorian period. And also through many other great personalities who were born under the same powerful configuration. Pasteur, for instance, had this conjunction with the Sun, Mercury and Venus.

It is quite possible that much of the cultural life of the nineteenth century and its predominant trends can be seen in this particular phenomenon. Indeed, Victorianism, as usually understood, would probably be regarded by the thoughtful astrologer as a Capricornian manifestation both on its better and less admirable sides.

Hitherto we have spoken only of conjunctions, though it is clear that oppositions, squares and trines all have their places, though less important ones. But the opposition of Uranus in Capricorn to Neptune in Cancer which was in operation from March 1, 1906, to October 28, 1910, is still with us, inasmuch as it occurs in so many nativities of those who are now between 40 and 50 years of age. So far as natal astrology is concerned, its operation will be most clear when it is angular or is closely involved with other bodies, and many a tragic map is on record in illustration of its extremely tensive action. As for the national life (and that of other nations) we see here the astrological index of the broken homes, widows and orphans of the 1914–18 war, and the children brought up without paternal guidance and correction. After the 1939 war it reappeared to affect another generation of children, and it must also be correlated with the housing shortage of the post-war years which is virtually world-wide. Psychologically this aspect did much to shake the moral standards of two generations, for the Cancer-Capricorn axis is important here. Cancer relates to instinctive and also inculcated habits, especially those acquired in early childhood; Capricorn relates to self-respect and moral character as it is consciously built up.

Dr. Barnardo, in an earlier period, was shocked to find a number of homeless children sleeping under the London arches; what would he have thought of hundreds of thousands, even millions, of homeless persons, of all ages, either lost in the maelstrom of war or ruthlessly dragged from their familiar and happy surroundings to pine and perish in remote and more or less desert places, at the will of some Nazi official, himself the slave of a system even more pitiless than himself? Astrologers might have foreseen *something* of this from the opposition we are now studying; but none of us would ever have ventured to predict the extent of this misery.

Uranus and Neptune may be "transcendental" planets, or "mystical" or "higher octaves"; but in the present state of man's unfoldment they *can* be indicative, in certain formations, of truly difficult tendencies.

We come finally to the conjunctions of Neptune and Pluto, which are rare indeed, occurring at about 500-year intervals. The last was in 1890–91, so that persons born under it were adult by 1914 and near 50 at the time of the Second Great War. It would be mere speculation to discuss the significance of such a rare phenomenon, but it could scarcely be fortunate.

On the other hand (to revert for a moment) the long-continued trine of Uranus to Neptune, first from Taurus to Virgo and later from Gemini to Libra, whilst it seems to have done nothing to alleviate the circumstances of the Second Great War, will probably produce some very interesting and helpful results as those born under it grow to maturity from about 1960 onwards. It seems to point to great advances in physical science; and the passage of the trine from earth signs to airy ones may point to discoveries which will bring into much closer harmony the spheres of the physical and metaphysical. The philosophical implications of Einstein's discoveries have not yet been worked out.

CHAPTER THREE

THE MATERIAL EMPLOYED

Part Two: *Stations. Comets. Ingresses. The Nativities of Important Persons.*

UNDER 2 (*c*) on page 16 above we have planetary Stations of which there are two kinds, those when a body is stationary to direct and those when it is stationary to retrograde. Of course the condition is purely apparent and the astronomical facts underlying it can easily be understood by means of a simple diagram on paper. This is not the place to explain such elementary matters.

In natal astrology there is a fair measure of agreement that a stationary planet is more powerful than one that is in apparent motion; but such questions cannot really be tested in any scientific sense. It is, however, hardly to be questioned that when a planet is stationary upon a sensitive point in a horoscope, the transit is particularly powerful, or that when a planet goes stationary in the progressed (day to a year) horoscope, its action becomes very marked, according to its radical strength and the manner in which it is circumstanced in the progressed map.

In mundane astrology stations are chiefly studied in relation to important maps, either of nations or of important individuals, but it is possible (since the times of the stations are given in the ephemerides) to erect maps for these occurrences, for any special place under consideration, and if the planet should go stationary at the moment that it is upon an angle, the correlated events might well be conspicuous. But this condition would rarely occur.

It is perhaps worth mentioning that in August 1939 there were three malefic stations, viz., on the 13th, Saturn in 1° 16′ Taurus ; on the 23rd, Mars in 23° 55′ Capricorn ; on the 28th, Uranus in 21° 58′ Taurus. The signs do not appear particularly significant. The Saturn station is near Hitler's Sun and that of Uranus is in close opposition to its natal place in King George's geniture ; that of Mars is in close opposition to Uranus in the map of the German Empire (see page 31).

It is also strange that all three stations occurred when the sun was close to the meridian, namely at 11 hr. 40 min. p.m., 11 hr. 57 min. p.m., and 0 hr. 10 min. p.m.

It should be added that in July and August 1914 there were no malefic stations, nor in June-July 1870 (Franco-Prussian War). Hence it seems that no great value is to be attached to stations as such except in very unusual circumstances, and their chief interest is as a special and powerful kind of transit.

Probably, if one wished to write a popular essay on Astrology, Comets would figure largely in it, for, since time immemorial, they have struck the imagination of writers and common folk alike, and always they have been associated with disaster. We are not writing a popular treatise, but one may recall *Julius Cæsar* :

" When beggars die there are no comets seen ;
The heavens themselves blaze forth the death of princes."

Milton says of Satan that he

" stood
Unterrified, and like a comet burned
That fires the length of Ophiuchus huge
In th' arctic sky, and from his horrid hair
Shakes pestilence and war."

Perhaps the most famous of all astrological forecasts was that of the astronomer and astrologer Tycho Brahe, who, from a consideration of the comet of 1577, foretold that a prince from the north would lay waste Germany and vanish in 1632. These predictions were fulfilled in Gustavus Adolphus.

The late Sir James Jeans wrote (in *Through Space and Time*): " Before their true nature was understood comets were regarded as portents of evil, and, oddly enough, many of the most conspicuous appearances of comets seem to have coincided with, or perhaps just anticipated, important events in history." A commendable example of fair-mindedness.

When it comes to a scientific theory of Comets it is less easy to write. These bodies, as the reader is probably well aware, have parabolic orbits which carry them far out into space and then (usually) back to the near neighbourhood of the Sun. A number are well known and their re-appearance can be foretold accurately. But they have no respect for the ecliptic and appear in all parts of the sky. Hence it is not easy to determine what part of the globe is threatened by them, but presumably it would be the portion where they are most prominently visible. This scarcely yields much basis for scientific prognostication. Indeed if conspicuous comets were at all frequent they would be a great nuisance to the predictive astrologer and would be the *enfants terribles* of his work !

On the subject of Ingresses a great deal can be said. The word is applied to the entry of a body into a sign, and at one period of British astrology the four cardinal ingresses, when the Sun enters Aries, Cancer, Libra and Capricorn, were the main structure of " mundane " work.

One finds the pages of *Modern Astrology* strewn with these figures and *Old Moore's Almanac* still appears to rely largely upon them and the monthly lunations and full moon figures.

It has been suggested that ingresses of the Sun into all the signs might be used, as well as those for the entry of the planets into the signs, especially into Aries.

The figures are erected for the metropolis of the country under consideration.

At once we see the difficulty of depending too much on maps which zodiacally are the same the world over. If the Sun is opposed to Saturn in the London chart so will it equally be for Pekin and Lima. The only difference is in mundane location, and even so this is not always great. We have already elaborated this point when writing of eclipses.

The experience of examining many of these ingress maps for the 1939–45 period has convinced me that, unless an angle is nearly involved, they are of little importance except in the most general sense. They form a background ; that is all. One cannot safely predict from them save in language so general as to be of little value.

One can indeed introduce the doctrine of astro-geology and declare that if Mars, for example, is strong it will be good for all countries ruled by that planet, and so forth. But this writer regards the natal map of the country and of its ruler, if these can be ascertained with accuracy, as being *by far* the truer and more scientific basis for mundane prediction.

There is also the possibility of comparing the ingress maps with those of nations and eminent personages and treating any transits that are formed by the bodies in the ingress as being peculiarly significant.

Mention should be made of an ancient rule that the vernal ingress is significant for the whole year if a fixed sign rises, for six months if a common sign rises, and for three months if a cardinal ascends. It is doubtful if this should be applied very rigidly.

We will now consider two vernal ingresses, for 1914 and for 1939.

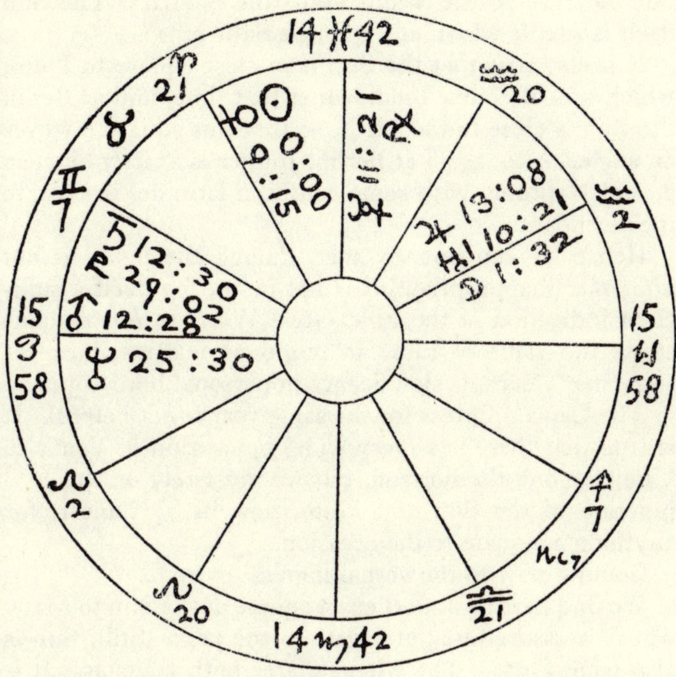

Map for the entry of the Sun into Aries, at 11 *hr.* 11 *min. a.m., G.M.T., on March* 21, 1914, *at London*

It will be agreed, the writer believes, that this is hardly the figure that one would expect to herald the beginning of the era of ruthless war and political knavery and oppression that has actually been in full spate ever since August 1914.

It is true that two malefics are near the ascendant (at least at London) and the ruler of the map is on cusp 8 (Placidus). Jupiter and Uranus are also in the 8th house, but they are sextile Venus and trine Saturn ! The Sun itself is sextile Moon and quintile Saturn.

It is also true that the Sun is in close square to Pluto, which was of course unknown at that time, and at Berlin the Sun is close to the M.C., so that this square involves an angle. Also, again at Berlin, Jupiter is exactly on cusp 8, and Neptune, with some southern latitude, is close to the ascendant.

Hence we can but say that, though the figure is not *altogether* inappropriate, it is not in and by itself a sufficient indication of the First Great War. It *does* demonstrate the value of Pluto in mundane matters, however some may query its significance in personal horoscopes.

The Cancer ingress for the same year is not helpful. It is true that there is a (very wide) opposition of Venus to Uranus along the horizon, but we must rely on the conjunction of the Sun and Pluto, now in 0½ Cancer, for anything adequate to the occasion.

Coming now to the vernal ingress for 1939.

We find here an almost exact square of the Sun to Mars, which is assuredly appropriate to the year. Still, Sun is also trine Pluto. The Moon shares both contacts. It is not a good map, but under a belief in its predominant importance I announced at the current Harrogate Convention that war was improbable ; the Sun square Mars seemed to me rather indicative of the re-armament that was at that time under way. The position of Venus in the 8th sextile the ruler of that house and Mercury, though also square Uranus, appeared reassuring. Here was an example of faulty judgment much to be regretted, for it was widely reported in the northern press.

Thus our judgment on these cardinal ingresses is not altogether a flattering one. They have been weighed in the balance and found wanting; or else this must be

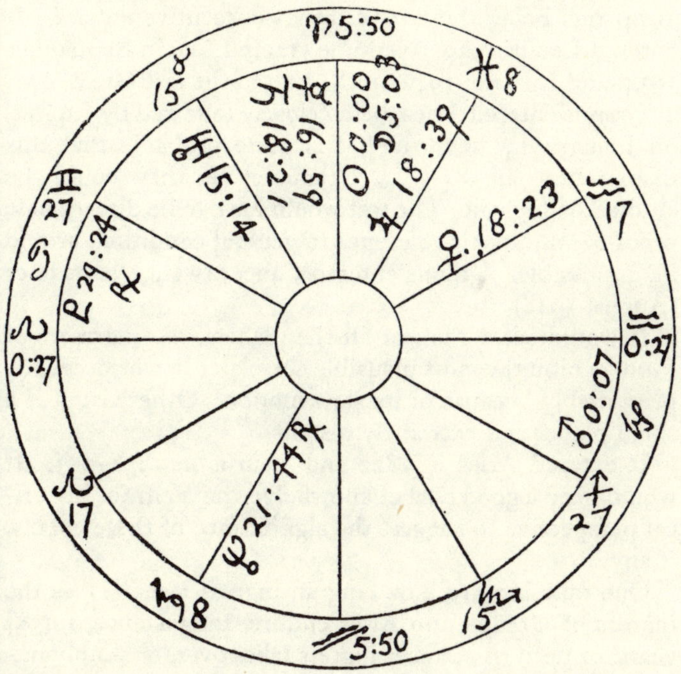

The above is the horoscope for the Vernal Ingress, at London, at 0 hr. 29 min. p.m., G.M.T., March 21, 1939

asserted of those who used them, i.e., that the maps are informative but have been badly read. But that would condemn too many able astrologers. I prefer to think that my forerunners in this field were capable, but too bound by tradition to seek and find better ways.

Besides the solar ingresses there are those of the planets, the times of which, very unfortunately, are not stated in the most widely used ephemerides.

The entry of Pluto into Cancer last occurred in May 1914, this being the last of three consecutive entries. It entered Leo in 1939. Neptune entered Leo in September 1914, and Libra in 1942, in the heat of the last Great War.

Uranus entered Aries, being closely followed by Jupiter, on January 13, 1928, and it is quite probable that this inaugurated an 84-year Uranus-cycle that could be studied with profit. The test would have to be directional; proof of validity by reference to general conditions would be impossible. Uranus entered Cancer twenty years later (August 1948).

It would seem that, of all the planets, the ingresses of Pluto exhibit the most plausible correlates in world-events, presumably because of its slow motion. Otherwise it is a small planet and extremely distant.

It entered Aries in 1822 and Taurus in 1851–2–3. It would need a good deal of knowledge and a gift for historical perspective to suggest the significance of these events, if any.

One may inquire how long an ingress lasts. Does the ingress of Uranus into Aries endure, for instance, for 84 years, or until the Cancer ingress takes over, or simply until the Taurus ingress?

In any case it would be an intricate task to follow the outworkings of several concurrently operative ingress horoscopes.

This seems a practical reason for seeking other and better methods of judgment.

But, to take one example, the Mars-cycle which began

in 1938 and covered the outbreak of the Hitler war showed the red planet in close conjunction with Saturn. But the cycle which began on July 2, 1941, and which covered Pearl Harbour, the fall of Singapore, and indeed the principal disasters of the Pacific war, showed Mars in close trine to Venus and in weak sextile to Jupiter; and the cycle which began on May 3, 1945, as the world war drew to its close, showed Mars opposed to Neptune and in square to Saturn!

3. Our next consideration, about which a very great deal could be written, is that of the nativities of important persons in their relation to Political Astrology.

It is traditional that the map of the Monarch, both natal and progressed, throws light upon the general character and periodic changes of the national life; and this seems true to-day and to include also the horoscopes of presidents, even when these are more or less figure-heads.

The point may at once be made that all these people have their personal lives. They suffer, for example, illnesses and bereavements like other folk. They get married, happily or otherwise. They have children.

How then distinguish between these purely personal events and those of national importance?

This is a serious objection and nevertheless it is not a crushing one. Important directions in royal horoscopes do normally appear to have a national concomitant, and conversely, important national events are usually shown in the royal genitures.

It was said that the theme of George V did not indicate the 1914 war. But that was because, at that time, the invaluable one-degree and radix measures were not in use even in this country—they are still apparently ignored by non-British students. The direction Venus to Uranus was almost exact by the one degree measure. Furthermore, there were strong multiple transits, and above all (though astrologers could not know this) Pluto was just entering the 4th house by transit.

It is reasonable to suppose that in royal nativities the 4th house and the 10th are particularly related to national affairs.

We give below the natus of His late Majesty King George VI.

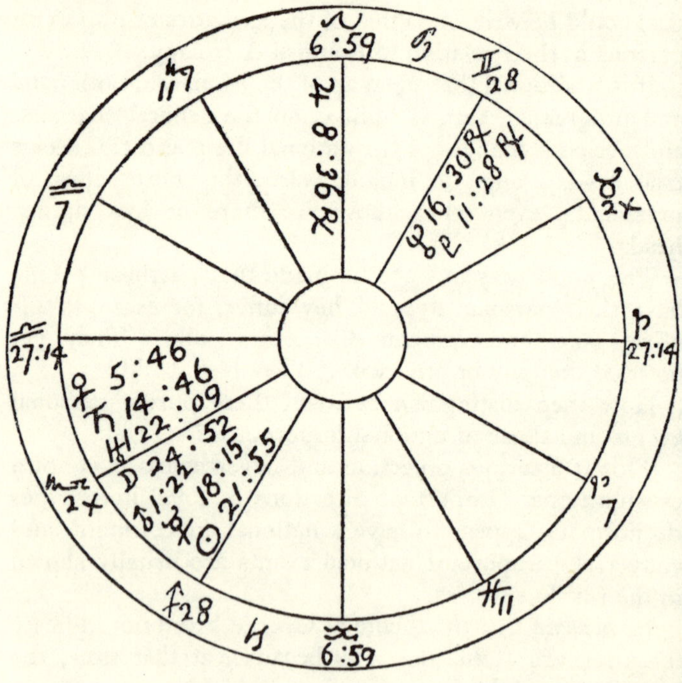

Geniture of H.M. King George VI, born at Sandringham, 3.05 a.m., G.M.T., December 14, 1895. Method of Placidus

It is easy to see in this figure the danger of heavy loss of property through war, for the 2nd house is afflicted by bodies in Scorpio, and Uranus and the Moon are squared by Saturn in the 1801 horoscope. Further, Jupiter, though its mundane position is so strong, is opposed to Mars in the 1066 figure (see page 25); in fact they are only 12′ from exactitude.

If we take the Moon as ruling the 10th (as it does by equal house division) the danger is magnified.

Not only was there great loss of property through the blitz but also the loss of the Indian Empire, Burma and Ceylon—loss, that is, in the sense that they ceased in any way to be British possessions. This took place when the progressed Sun was in square to radical Saturn; and this direction also covered the (first) austerity period. The square of the Sun to progressed Saturn follows at the end of the present year (1951) and renewed privations are already in sight.

The same directions correlate with tension between Britain and the Jews (a Saturn race) and Russia (under Aquarius).

During the War, Mars was around the ascendant by axial direction, whilst the ascendant was opposed to Pluto by one degree increment.*

Progressed Sun opposition radical Jupiter dated to the outbreak of war with the Japanese. Progressed Mercury squared Uranus and the Moon during the war.

Regressive (= pre-natal) Mars came to conjunction radical ascendant in 1945, which seems inappropriate, although regressive Venus was sextile radical Uranus. As a general rule regressions are almost, if not quite, as significant as progressions, or post-natal secondaries.

*If the above ascendant is exactly right, the asc. was opposed to Pluto in the spring of 1940, when the so-called " phoney war " ended.

But progressed Sun was in trine to Pluto, radical and progressed, in 1944–45.

Its trine to Neptune coincided with the abundant financial help given to the United Kingdom by the Americans.

In fine, one must admit strict limits to the trustworthiness of this class of map.

So long as a monarch identifies his life with that of his nation, so long there may be a close relationship between his horoscopic conditions and the national welfare. The above example justifies this assertion.

But an unpopular ruler must necessarily be considered differently. In *his* case a downfall, shown in his natus by " bad " directions, would be an excellent thing for his country; he would in fact " leave his country for his country's good."

Another consideration is that a king or president may die or abdicate and any prognostications founded on his geniture will immediately lack substantial basis.

As the true maps of the various countries are ascertained it is probable that less and less use will be made, in political astrology, of this type of horoscope, for the reasons stated.

The two next nativities are given because of their importance and the interest taken in them.

It is clear that the first is a difficult horoscope, the ruler Saturn being elevated, it is true, but being also square Mars-Jupiter opposed to Neptune. The best feature, though rather negative, is that neither Light is afflicted.

The conjunction of Mars, ruling the southern meridian, with Jupiter points to accession, but the opposition of both to Neptune indicates, at some period, a withdrawal from power and responsibility.

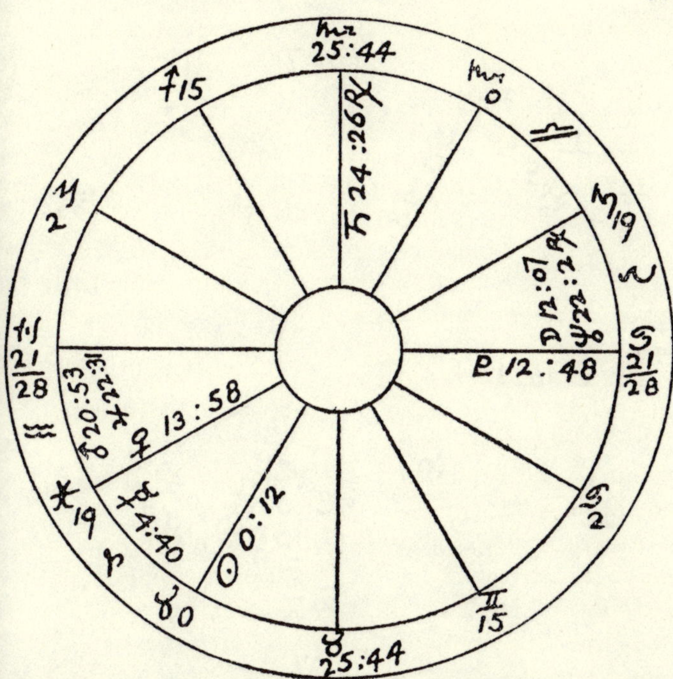

*Nativity of Queen Elizabeth, born at Bruton Street, London, W.*1, 1.40 *a.m., G.M.T., April* 21, 1926. *Placidian cusps*

When we compare this nativity with the 1066 map on page 25 we see an interesting set-up. The 1066 ascendant, 22 Aries, is in favourable contact with Mars, Jupiter and Neptune in the Queen's geniture, but Neptune, since it is in exact semisextile with the ascendant in the 1066 horoscope, is in square to these bodies, and opposed to Saturn. This would seem good for personal popularity, but it clearly indicates present economic difficulties, for Neptune 1066 is in Taurus.

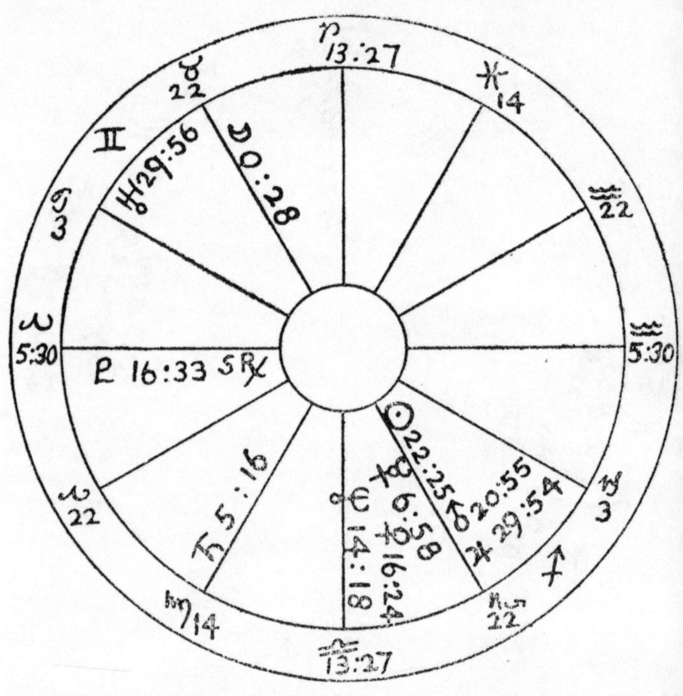

Geniture of Prince Charles, born at Buckingham Palace, at 9.14 *p.m., G.M.T., November* 14, 1948. *Placidian cusps*

This is clearly a rather favourable horoscope, though whether it is of a royal character is possibly more open to question, since Jupiter is virtually cadent, no less than six bodies being in the obscure N.W. quadrant. The opposition of Jupiter and Uranus is very close. The conjunction of Venus and Neptune on the lower meridian is interesting ; however, they are sextile Mars and Pluto.

The Moon is remarkably strong, being exalted, angular,

in grand trine with Jupiter and Saturn, and sextile Uranus.

If the native should ascend the throne it would probably be a happy event for the country. But his ☉ is closely opposed to 1066 ♆!

Perhaps it would be best to sum up the value of these maps by saying that it is best to use them in a negative sense. That is to say, a monarch might have such a direction as Sun square Mars and it might have an almost entirely personal effect, pointing to illness or accident. But on the other hand it seems improbable that a country would be involved in war unless there were some fairly clear concomitant direction in the royal horoscope.

When we come to dictators such as Mussolini or Hitler, who virtually hold the fate of the country in their hands, the concomitance will probably be very marked.

In Hitler's case it is known that he was, at any rate at first, guided by astrological advice, only discarding his astrologers when they could no longer tell him what he wished to hear.

It seems plain that he deliberately started the war when he was under Sun trine Uranus radical and Venus (ruler) trine Jupiter. Such directions might have deceived any astrologer, who would have thought that no one would begin hostilities when his ruler was in good aspect to Jupiter. It is true that regressive Mars was going to square Moon and Jupiter radical, but these were not exact. Actually these directions enabled Hitler to make great conquests at little cost to Germany. Happily for the world, "good" directions do not last very long, and the slow relentless pressure of Saturn to square Mars, exact at the time of El Alamein and Stalingrad, wore the Nazis down. At the time of the dictator's death regressive Venus was opposed to regressive Uranus and regressive Sun was going to the quadrature of Pluto.

We omit reference to the angular (axial) directions as the exact time of birth is a matter of doubt.

The above demonstrates that when astrology is being consciously used, judgment must take account of this circumstance. It is said that the Russians are very proficient in certain branches of our art. It would be a matter of interest to hear how they reconcile its facts with their dialectic materialism. It is quite possible that in due course this will be explained to us.

Mussolini may also have been advised astrologically, for he entered the war which was to close so disastrously for him and for Italy, when his progressed Sun was trine Pluto. Progressed Mars was going from conjunction radical Jupiter to conjunction radical Venus.

Regressive Sun had passed conjunction radical Mars, strangely, but was going to the conjunction of radical Moon and Saturn—it was this last direction that brought him down. Regressed Saturn also went over Pluto in 1942.

Marshal Stalin has of course never been the titular head of the U.S.S.R., but his map (which is speculative as regards the hour of birth) indicates the war fairly clearly. Progressed Uranus came to opposition radical Jupiter, probably in 1940 and progressed Mercury came to opposition Uranus, radical and progressed. Progressed Sun square progressed Mars did not become exact till later, probably in 1944. Another difficult direction was Neptune conjunction its radical place.

The end of the war seems to have been denoted by strong favourable aspects formed by progressed Mercury. Assuming a Scorpio ascendant this planet rules the 10th*

*Marshal Stalin has considerable personal charm and Venus rising in Scorpio seems a fair conjecture.

We do not propose to add further examples of this class, but would close by repeating that their value must depend on the extent to which the ruler and the nation can be identified.

But it is worth pointing out that this identification is by no means limited to rulers. *All* patriotic people do to some degree make this identification ; and, even apart from patriotism, the vicissitudes of the national fortunes affect most people quite intimately nowadays. Of course a state of war may be highly profitable to some persons and indeed to whole trades, even apart from deliberate profiteering. Abnormal conditions create abnormal demands —and the reverse. Some capitalists thrive on war ; others are ruined by it or are harassed to the verge of lunacy by restrictive ordinances. Some can sell their products many times over ; others could do so, if they were able to produce them ; others find their goods are no longer in demand at all. But if we take the case of the plain citizen who loves his native land, we shall find that there is a fair correspondence between his directions and the really important fluctuations in the national welfare.

However, it is (once again to repeat ourselves) the true national maps that should be the main basis of Political Astrology.

CHAPTER FOUR

THE MATERIAL EMPLOYED

Part Three. *Inceptionals, The Horoscopes of Nations. Some Special Horoscopes. The New Year Figure.*

In a sense all astrological maps are inceptional maps, for they are cast for some beginning. A chart for the vernal equinox is the beginning of a cycle. A nativity is the beginning of a life. A horary question is asked for the time when some project is mooted, or first enters one's mind.

I use the term to denote the many kinds of figure that are cast for the commencement of human projects, using that word in a very wide sense.

Such maps may be for non-substantial projects, i.e., the "birth of an idea," or they may be for substantial events, such as the laying of a foundation stone. Most human enterprises naturally have both aspects. First comes the decision to build a city or town hall or bridge, next comes the cutting of the first turf, the laying of the first brick, or as the case may be. Which figure would be the more valuable? This question would be difficult to answer, but perhaps it is logical to believe that the former, being first in time, would predominate over the second.

In Political Astrology we are usually concerned, however, with the latter, because we rarely know when a political idea is first conceived.

In considering such a thing, for instance, as the famous Schumann Plan we cannot know when M. Schumann first thought of it. We can know when he made his first public announcement about it, and we could also know the time when (if ever) it became embodied in documentary form and was formally signed. Even so, we often find with treaties that they are first signed and are ratified much later !

The term " election " is used to denote these types of map when their time is deliberately chosen or elected. But it is questionable whether this has often occurred in political matters, though in these times one never knows.

It would be possible to make other classifications of Inceptionals.

For example, some are astronomical. The Vernal Equinox maps and other ingresses are really inceptional figures, of a cyclic character. The New Year Map (of which we shall have a good deal to say later) is a cyclic map, but the cycle is artificial or arbitrary rather than astronomical. Others, such as the birth-time of nations, are not astronomical at all, but are either fortuitous (humanly speaking) or are, or will be, conscious elections.

We have already discussed some of these and printed the national horoscopes of certain countries. We cannot supply many, because so few are at all reliable.

Again, nowadays national maps are quite as subject to sudden obliteration as those of kings, presidents, dictators and other leaders, with this added difference, that one can tell when one of these is dead or at least dethroned, but it is not always easy to assert that a given national map has ceased to have validity.

Thus, has the new Japanese constitution superseded the map of 1889? Did the New Constitution granted the Russian people in 1936 in any way oust the original map for the U.S.S.R.? Did the secession of Southern Ireland affect the validity of our 1801 figure (apparently not)?

National Horoscopes

We will now table the maps or possible maps of some of the principal countries of the present world.

European

That of the *United Kingdom* has been already given and seems reliable.

We have also given the maps for the *Coronation of William I* and for the *Union of England and Scotland*.

These are not easy to test as the data are not available for directions. The 1066 horoscope certainly appears to be trustworthy, and it is often possible to make sound deductions from the correspondences between it and the nativities of British monarchs as to the success or otherwise of their reigns, and the destiny of the nation during their terms of office.

It will be seen that there are striking correspondences between the 1066 and 1707 maps, the two Moon-positions being closely opposed to each other, whilst the place of Uranus in the 1066 figure (of the importance of which point we have already spoken) is in square to both.

France

The data for the Third Republic are 4.36 p.m., G.M.T., September 4, 1870, Paris.

We give opposite the map of the Fourth Republic:

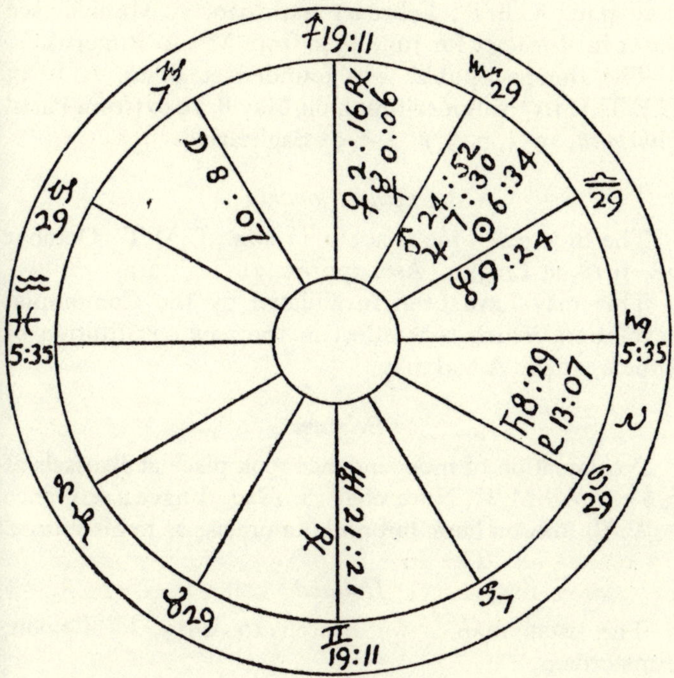

Map of the Fourth Republic (France) 2.40 p.m., L.M.T., October 30, 1946, Paris

Germany

We have given the map of the Empire (see page 31).

The German Republic was founded at Berlin, at 1.30 p.m., C.E.T., November 9, 1918.

The Nationalist Socialist State was established at 11 a.m., C.E.T., January 30, 1933, at Berlin (from Goering's book *Germany Reborn*). This seems like an election. The Nazi Party is said to have been founded at

7.29 p.m., C.E.T., February 24, 1920, at Munich (see letter in *Astrology* for June 1940 from Mr. A. Ruperti).

The Bundesrepublik was founded at Bonn, at 10.55 C.E.T. (11.55 summer time), on May 8, 1949 (from Paris' *Jahrbuch*, 1951, p. 37). Asc. 21 Sagittarius.

Czecho-Slovakia

The time given me is about 11 a.m., L.M.T., October 28, 1918, at Prague. Asc. approx. 21 Sagittarius.

This may have been invalidated by the Communist revolution, which took effect in the new constitution of June 9, 1948. A bad map.

Belgium

Proclamation of independence took place at Brussels at 3.6 p.m., G.M.T., November 18, 1830. I have a reference to V. E. Robson here, but nothing precise as to his source.

Holland

The usual map is for March 16, 1815, local noon, Amsterdam.

Spanish Republic

April 14, 1931, Madrid, 6.10 p.m., G.M.T. (?). From *Famous Nativities*; a very bad map presumably superseded by that of the Franco régime, as to which I have no details.

Poland

I have this under 10.30 a.m., November 14, 1918, Warsaw, but no reference. This may have been superseded by the map of the existing Communist régime.

Norway

Separation from Sweden, 10.30 a.m., C.E.T., June 7,

1905, Oslo. Data from *Times* of June 8, 1905. My original map was annotated " may be about half an hour later."

Hungary

Given in *Famous Nativities* as 1.17 p.m., L.M.T., March 1, 1920. This is noon, G.M.T. I do not know why so many astrologers, especially on the Continent, persist in stating times in L.M.T. The use of L.M.T. can be scrapped with great advantage—see Appendix I.

U.S.S.R.

The whole question of the true U.S.S.R. horoscope has been examined many times, but without definitive results. They celebrate their October Revolution on November 7. On that day, in 1917 at Leningrad, the Bolshevik Congress began to sit ; it continued to do so throughout the night, and resumed on the evening of the 8th. Proceedings terminated about 5.15 a.m. on the 9th, and thereafter wires were sent out declaring that the Bolshevik government had taken power (see Miss Gardiner's article *Two Revolutions*, Astrology Vol. XI, page 156, quoting Trotzky's account).

It is obvious that there is no indication here as to when the crucial resolution was put to the meeting and carried.

Miss Gardiner took the sending out of the telegrams as the decisive time and erected her map for 5.15 a.m., E.E.T., November 11, 1917, Leningrad. Libra 23 rises. But several other alternatives have been proposed.

It should be possible to determine the exact ascendant from the transit of Neptune through the last decan of Libra if that sign is in fact on the ascendant at all. Even then it might be on the 8th or 9th, but not on the 7th, because the Congress did not begin till the evening of that day.

Against all these possibilities it may be that the Russian

people, by adopting the 7th themselves, have, so to speak, created an artificial but operative figure for that day, perhaps at noon. This would probably be for Moscow, the present capital.

E. H. Troinski, of Berlin, has sent me a map for 10.45 p.m., L.M.T., Leningrad, November 7, which may have been the time the Congress began.

Mr. C. Hey, a careful American student of such matters, has 0.59 p.m., November 7, Leningrad.

Mr. Marshall Harmer has proposed 5 a.m., November 8.

It will be seen that the position is " fluid."

The true map should certainly show significant transits for June 22, 1941, when the Nazis attacked the Soviet Union, and in this connection a curious horoscope, published in the *British Journal of Astrology* for June–May 1933 by V. E. Robson and ascribed to a Belgian, M. Brahy, has some interest. For the opposition of Mars to Neptune which fell on June 23, 1941, falls on the meridian of this figure. But Miss Gardiner wrote that she could find no event whatsoever to justify this map, which is for September 15, 1917, local noon, Leningrad.

Italy

I have no data for the Republic, and several very uncertain ones for the Kingdom.

The Fascist State was inaugurated at 10 a.m., C.E.T., October 31, 1922, at Rome.

Asiatic

Burma

The declaration of independence (chosen by the astrologers) was made at 4.20 a.m., L. St. Time, January 4, 1948, Rangoon.

China

The Republic was established on January 1, 1912, at Pekin, and the time is given as midnight. There is some directional confirmation for this.

According to the *Astrological Magazine* (Bangalore) issue of March 1950, page 213, the People's Republic was set up at 3.15 p.m., October 1, 1949, at Pekin.

India

The Empire was proclaimed at noon, November 1, 1858, L.M.T., at Allahabad.

The Dominion came into existence at midnight, August 15, 1947, at New Delhi.

The Republic is said to have begun as from midnight, January 26, 1950, but it is also asserted that the true time was during the morning, when the Viceroy vacated his chair of office and the President took his place. See London *Daily Telegraph* for January 27.

Israel

The termination of the British mandate dates from midnight local standard time, May 14–15, 1948, as at Tel-Aviv.

The State was proclaimed on the afternoon of May 14, at Tel-Aviv ; this was done according to the *Times* 8 hours before the mandate officially terminated because Saturday is the Jewish Sabbath, i.e. at 4 p.m., May 14, one-hour summer time.

Japan

The old map, which appeared valid during the World War, was for 10.30 a.m., local standard time, February 11, 1889.

I have no later map.

Pakistan

The Dominion was set up at midnight 14–15 August, 1947, at Karachi.

Turkey

Time is stated at 8.30 p.m., local standard time, October 29, 1923, Ankara.

AFRICA

Egypt

According to the *B.J.A.*, June 1936, the time is 6.45 p.m., local standard time, March 15, 1922, Cairo.

THE AMERICAS

Argentine Republic

According to *World Astrology* the data are : noon (local mean ?) July 9, 1816, at Tucuman.

Canada

In the *British Journal of Astrology*, October 1930, a map is given for March 29, 1867, noon, the position being : M.C. 7.13 ♈, Asc. 27.10♋, ☉ 8.33♈, ☽ 23.47♑, ☿ 3.28 ♈℞, ♀ 25.3♒, ♂ 18.49 ♋, ♃ 26.49 ♒, ♄ 23.34 ♏℞, ♅ 4.29 ♋℞, ♆ 12. 22 ♈, PL 13½ ♉.

I have also a figure given for noon, July 1, 1867, Ottawa. But the conjunctions of the Lights with Uranus seems rather too explosive to be acceptable.

United States

The map is uncertain, owing to doubt as to the time of the signing of the Declaration of Independence.

American astrologers are divided between two Gemini and a Libra rising map, with some adherents for Sagittarius rising.

Psychological qualities seem to point to a Gemini

ascendant, and ascendants of 8.47, 7.35 and 20.11 Gemini have been advocated. Those who favour Libra use an asc. of 13.32 of that sign All are for Philadelphia, July 4, 1776. The chart below is that of Mr. C. Hey.

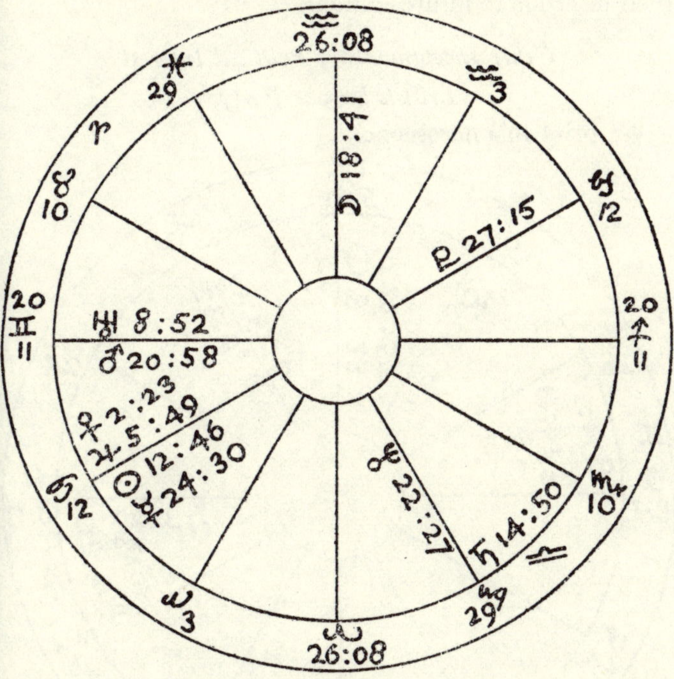

Horoscope for the United States of America, see 1940 *Year-Book of the American Federation of Astrologers*

From a psychological viewpoint it might seem that Uranus is more likely to be just rising in the national map than Mars, bearing in mind the great technical efficiency of the Americans, and their liking for gadgets and all sorts of mechanical devices.

It is much to be regretted that it is not possible to include a number of other national data and the author will be happy to receive trustworthy information, with full particulars as to sources, of this kind, with a view to their insertion in future editions.

Other Inceptionals of Political Interest

British Labour Party

We print this horoscope.

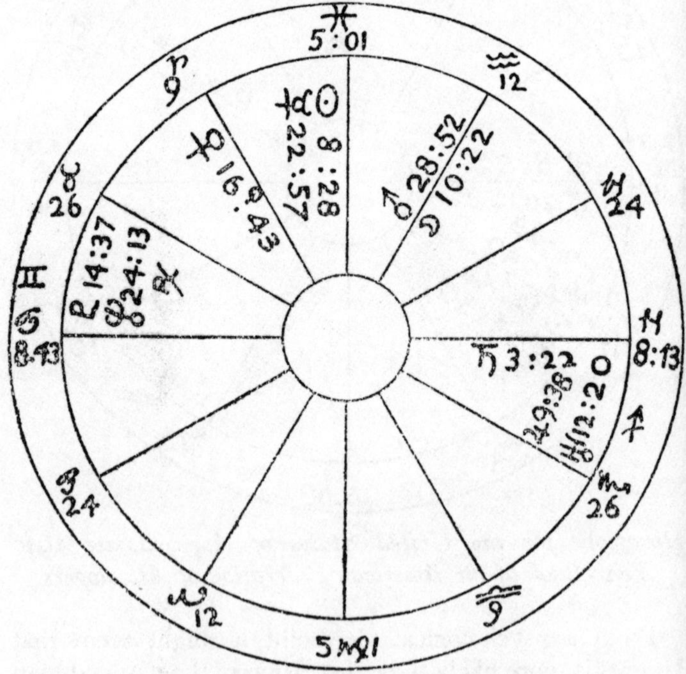

Map of British Labour Party, for midday, G.M.T., February 27, 1900, *London E.C.*4

This figure appears to yield reliable directions.

The United Nations Organisation (UNO)

This is said to come to birth at 4.45 p.m., E.S.T., October 24, 1945, at Washington, the positions being ;

M.C. 11.9 ♑, Asc. 20.02 ♈, ☉ 1.08 ♏, ☽ 22.33 ♊, ☿ 15.23 ♏, ♀ 7.07 ♎, ♂ 23.59 ♋, ♃ 12.50 ♎, ♄ 24.45 ♋, ♅ 17.02 ♊ ℞, ♆ 7.05 ♎, PL 11.43 ♌.

The malefics in Cancer reflect the first great divergence in regard to the admission of Communist China.

I also have a date for the signing of the Charter at San Francisco : 3.30 Pacific Coast Time, April 25, 1945. This is from the *Astrological Review* (Astrologers' Guild of America), November 1949.

I have also data for the opening of UNO at London, at 4.02 p.m., January 10, 1946.

This is an almost incredibly bad figure.

New Year Horoscopes

The use of these figures appears to have been first suggested by a correspondent to *Modern Astrology* in Alan Leo's days. He based his suggestion on the fact that, at midnight of the old year, many thousands are in effect asking a horary question : what will the new year bring ?

Otherwise the moment of the birth of the new year is of course purely artificial and lacks all astronomical reality. In the view of some astrologers this would nevertheless not constitute a decisive objection to the validity of such maps. To discuss this point would take us into the world of Metaphysics, but we may refer to the *Dhammapada* : " All that we are is the result of what we have thought ; it is compounded of our thoughts, made up of our thoughts." It is possible that man may himself create valid figures if the faith that he can do so be present.

These figures should be cast for the capital city of the country under examination and they will differ little (except for the position of the Moon) all the world over, since the metropolis is usually close to the standard time-meridian of the country.

The general character of the maps, then, will constitute a great limitation on their value, in themselves. They will only be of use for general purposes, unless we can relate them to " local " figures, such as those of national leaders or of countries or governments.

The N.Y. horoscope for 1914 showed Mars in M.C. opposed to the Sun, and Jupiter was closely opposed to Neptune. Venus, ruler, was going to opposition Pluto (close).

The 1915 figure was very destructive. The Moon opposed Mercury, Sun and Mars, and she was conjoined with Pluto.

1916 was better, but Sun was going to opposition Saturn on M.C. In 1917 the configurations are worst of all, as a glance at the ephemeris will show. Mars and Mercury oppose Saturn, the Moon and Jupiter are in quadrature to them.

1918, though it was the year of peace to us, was also a year of revolution and of bloodshed in many lands. Venus, ruler, is with Uranus and the Moon opposes both closely.

Now as regards collating these figures with nativities here are the main correspondences for World War One. The relevant radical positions are given, and against them the places in the N.Y. chart that are in relation with them

	Radicals	*New Year* 1914
George V	Jupiter 25.40 Sag.	Mercury 26 Sag.
	Uranus 28.38 Gem.	Venus 29½ Sag.
	Mars 5.35 Leo	Uranus 6 Aq.
	Sun 12.26 Gem.	Saturn 13 Gem.
	Moon 1.03 Libra	PL 0 Cancer

	Radicals	*New Year* 1914
Franz Josef	Venus 24 Cancer	Jup. 25 Cancer
		Nep. 27 Cancer
	Uranus 8 Aq.	Uranus 6 Aq.
Albert	Mars 26 Sag.	Merc. 26 Sag.
		Venus $29\frac{1}{2}$ Sag.
	Asc. $14\frac{1}{2}$ Cancer	Mars $16\frac{1}{2}$ Cancer
Tsar	Uranus $10\frac{1}{2}$ Cancer	Mars $16\frac{1}{2}$ Cancer
	Venus $12\frac{1}{2}$ Cancer	
	Nep. 16 Aries	
Kaiser	Nep. 23 Pisces	Merc. 26 Sag.
	Mars 27 Pisces	Venus $29\frac{1}{2}$ Sag.
	Jupiter 12 Gem.	Saturn 13 Gem.
	Sun 7 Aq.	Uranus 6 Aq.
	Saturn 9 Leo	
	Merc. 13 Cap.	Mars 16 Cancer

The Maps for World War Two are also destructive, though the emphasis seems mainly on Uranus.

1939 : Sun sq. setting Saturn; Mars opposition Uranus.
1940 : Moon conj. Neptune, both opposed to Mars.
1941 : Mars opposition Uranus, both squared by Moon.
1942 : Saturn conj. Uranus, both squared by Venus.
1943 : Mars opp. Saturn, wide.
1944 : Mars conj. Uranus, Venus going to opposition.
1945 : Mercury conj. Mars, square Jupiter, but sextile Venus.

We will not correlate the 1939 figure with many of the principal actors in the drama of war that ensued. But the opposition Mars $12\frac{1}{2}$ Scorpio to Uranus 14 Taurus narrowly affects our King's Saturn, $14\frac{3}{4}$ Scorpio, and Hitler's famous Venus-Mars conjunction in the 17th degree of

Taurus. Stalin has Mars in 13 Taurus, and Churchill Mercury square Uranus falls from 18 Scorpio to 15 Leo. Roosevelt had a conjunction of Neptune and Jupiter in the 14th and 17th degrees of Taurus.

Students must decide for themselves how far these figures are, as a class, worth while. It is not difficult to find years that began badly and yet produced no world wars. For example, 1910 could hardly be excelled for evil if we judge solely by the new year figure.

But one cannot judge "solely" by any figure; one must consider them always in the light of the historical context. In 1910 the world is still infinitely more stable than it has since become.

Even so, 1910 saw the annexation of Korea by Japan and historians may see in this, and in other inconspicuous events of that year, the sowing of seeds that led later to "red ruin and the breaking up of laws."

Those who argue that because a tensive map was followed by a great war, therefore every equally tensive map should be followed by an equally destructive war lack both astrology and sense. It is not as simple as all that.

A generation ago astrologers sought to forecast the fate of the year by the vernal equinox figure, supplemented by the lunations and eclipses and little else. They failed miserably and went from blunder to blunder. Whether the new year map is better than the Vernal Ingress horoscope, or whether it is any use at all, I leave to students to decide for themselves. That it is more than one landmark out of many no sensible astrologer would contend.

CHAPTER FIVE

HISTORICAL CYCLES AND NEWLY FOUND PLANETS

CYCLES have played a large part in some work on Mundane Astrology and the succession of "periods," ruled by the planets, is a mainstay of Hindu predictive astrology, both natal and general.

In the West we have heard about the so-called Aquarian Age, which is to follow that of Pisces and for some unexplained reason is to be so much pleasanter to inhabit, until the very mention of this term fills the careful astrologer with apprehension. For it is questionable whether many who talk about it, and even some of those who write about it, understand what is meant. One writer even explained that we were now in the last decanate of Pisces, that of Scorpio, and so were getting a truly sanguinary time! Of course the motion of the vernal equinox is retrograde and so passes backwards through Pisces, from the third to the second and the first decan of the *constellation* Pisces.

Not sign, of course; the vernal equinox point, being by the very nature of things the beginning of the zodiac of signs, cannot possibly be anything, in terms of the signs, than 0 Aries. It is the passage of this 0 Aries through constellation Pisces into constellation Aquarius that will herald the "Aquarian Age."

But whether a constellation in any way resembles the corresponding sign, or whether it may be divided into decanates, who can say?

However, it is certain that periods or epochs do occur and can be correlated with the signs. This will, I believe, be quite clear to those who have the astrological knowledge that will indicate to them what should be looked for.

These periods are not only intensely interesting historically, but they also provide a background for all social and political studies, dominating as they do the entire life of their times.

I cannot claim to any special historical knowledge, least of all of foreign countries, but the following is given as an indication of a method which better-informed students may care to follow. It is reprinted from *Astrology* for December, 1947.

It must be strongly emphasised that these periods may have no connection at all with precession or the constellations.

" In considering the effects, if any, of the passage of the First Point through the constellations, two main questions arise (1) have the zodiacal constellations the same values respectively as the twelve signs and (2) how are their dimensions to be determined ?

As regards (1) it is logical to suppose that the answer is in the affirmative ; the zodiacal constellations have the same values, if any, as the twelve signs of the zodiac. As for (2) we all know that the twelve signs comprise each an arc of 30° of the ecliptic. But the areas of the constellations were never settled with anything like this precision until quite modern times and are quite different one from another : therefore it would indeed be difficult to assert with assurance when the First Point will enter the constellation Aquarius and the so-called and much-heralded Aquarian Age will begin.

In this article we are treating the whole matter empirically.

The First Point travels round the ecliptic in about 25,868 years. Divided by twelve, this yields periods of 2,156 years. But such a period is still too long, in relation to recorded history, to enable us to make any very useful or convincing correlations. A few points, sufficiently intriguing, suggest themselves, but they will not carry us far enough.

But if we carry our duodenary division further, divide 2,156 by 12 once more and obtain epochs of about 180 years, we may find ourselves able to carry out some useful researches into the correspondences that may be found between these epochs and the accepted values of the twelve zodiacal signs (or constellations).

I propose to take the commencement of the Christian Era as a starting-point and to limit myself, almost exclusively, to European history. It is quite possible that other cultures have other datum-points and in any case I confess that to attempt to deal in this fashion with world-history would be quite beyond my powers, and in any case much beyond the possible scope of the present article.

It is well known that, traditionally, the First Point of Aries is said to have entered the constellation of the Fishes about A.D. 1, thus inaugurating what I am now calling a period of 2,156 years which has been under a Piscean signature. There is a good deal of evidence to support this theory, into which we need not enter, since we are now to consider the epochs of approximately 180 years.

But we are immediately confronted with the question as to whether we are to take these epochs in the usual order of the signs, or whether, following the example of the retrograde precessional movement, we are to take them in the reverse order. Furthermore, in either case, should we commence each period with an epoch coming under Aries, or coming under the same sign as that which rules the period? Thus, will the Piscean period start with an Aries or a Pisces 180-year epoch?

From the standpoint of logical consistency perhaps there is something to be said for taking the signs in the reverse order; whereas it hardly seems as if there is anything to choose, from this standpoint, between the other alternatives, i.e., beginning always with Aries or with the sign of the period. Actual consideration of the facts has convinced me that we must begin the Piscean period with an Aries epoch and continue through the signs in their customary order.

I hope that I shall be able to make out at least a *prima facie* case in support of this view. It will be found, however, that the earlier epochs are not as clearly defined as the later are. It is often asserted by the uninformed that only primitive and ignorant people respond to planetary indications, but actually this is a totally incorrect view. From the stone up to the most highly developed man there is an increasing degree of responsivity. Naturally the highly developed man responds *differently* from the boor, but he responds more, not less. The way to lessen one's responsivity is to lead as far as may be a completely humdrum and routine life, inwardly and outwardly; in a word, to empty one's life as far as possible of all content. Even so, the effort may be unsuccessful. As with the individual, so with man collectively. As he advances in unfoldment, so planetary response becomes more obvious. We feel some doubts as to the first epoch being under Aries; we shall find it harder to question that we are now under Aquarius.

We begin, then, from A.D. 0 or thereabouts. The exact date of Jesus' birth is uncertain, but a matter of a few years is of small importance, for *Natura non agit per saltum* and we shall always find that one epoch tends to pass somewhat gradually into the next.

Our first epoch, which we place under Aries, extends from A.D. 0 to A.D. 180.

The latter date is highly interesting, for it is that of the death of the philosopher-emperor Marcus Aurelius, probably one of the best and wisest men ever to occupy a throne. Now, it is from that very event that Gibbon dates the commencement of the Decline and Fall of the Roman Empire.

This first epoch covers the period of the Cæsars and their successors Nerva, Trajan, Hadrian and the two Antonines. It was a period during which absolute power lay in the hands of one man and that power was hardly disputed, although there was a very brief civil war after the death of Galba. It was an age of complete despotism except in so far as this was tempered by the fear of assassination or military revolt.

This agrees well enough with Aries.

But we find under each of the fire-signs an element of renewed vitality, often showing itself in external grandeur, and so this epoch begins with an Augustan Age.

The next epoch (A.D. 180 to 360) seems more difficult to associate with Taurus, though one is immediately reminded of the extraordinary, though impermanent, spread of the cult of Mithras throughout the Empire. In the Mithraic Mysteries the Bull figures largely.

For the rest, it is a period of miserable intellectual sterility (the one name to mention with honour being that of Plotinus, the Neo-Platonist) and of military revolutions and defeats at the hands of the barbarians until the establishment, in 284, of what it is the fashion nowadays to call the sultanate of Diocletian. Of this Dean Inge writes: 'The advent of the Dark Ages was deferred only by the amazing cast-iron despotism of Diocletian and his successors, which saved the empire from a welter of savagery at the cost of establishing a bureaucratic caste-system ' (*Philosophy of Plotinus*, page 32).

This sounds true to Taurus, and Dean Inge, in the same work, gives us another pointer. He speaks of ' the great prestige of the revived Persian empire in the third century '—now, Persia is under Taurus, and it is very natural that in any given epoch, countries that come under the same sign-value as the epoch will in some respect experience an augmentation.

We may recall that Britain, though by no means barbarous before the advent of the Romans, was largely unknown to the rest of the world until the Roman conquest at the time of Claudius in the Aries epoch.

Two other features of this epoch deserve mention. The bloody wars, insurrections and assassinations must be ascribed to polarity—Scorpio in lieu of Taurus. The great and genuine religious revival is another matter. It cannot be denied that there was an immense change in this respect during the third century, and most of us would call the change an advance. This was contemporary with the spread of Christianity but does not seem to have been entirely due to it ; in fact, it might be truer to say that the spread of Christianity was one of the aspects of the new craving for moral purity, sanctity and communion with the Divine. In this connection the life of Apollonius written during the period under consideration by one Philostratus, is interesting. Apollonius was a Pythagorean who lived about the time of Jesus but Philostratus' portrait is drawn according to what was expected of a religious leader in the third century. It is a feeble portrait, too regarded as a piece of descriptive writing ; but it shows that an ideal of saintliness had come into men's minds that would have seemed strange and unintelligible to the pagans of a century before.

Now, how we can derive this development from the Taurus significance, I hardly know ; and it is perhaps more likely that (especially as it is a feature that will remain and unfold right up to our own times) it has nothing to do with the Taurus epoch, but springs from the Piscean signature of the entire period of 2,160 years.

In examining any astrological theory of cycles we must expect sufficient evidence that it has a basis in truth, but we must not expect it to cover all aspects of the periods under review, for there must inevitably be numerous other ' influences ' at work at any particular time. Above all, there must be the Horoscope of Man, of which we have no knowledge whatever, but which must certainly be operative.

Gemini assumes domination at A.D. 360, and we look, not in vain, for evidence of duality. In 364 Valentinian, by bestowing the Eastern part of his realms upon his brother, for the first time divided the Roman Empire into two. The final division came about a generation later.

We look also for literary activity, and it is true that there is a certain renaissance of letters of which Inge writes that Ausonius and Claudian made it ' not undistinguished.'

Perhaps the most striking thing about this period, from the general European point of view, was the dominance of the Germanic races. During the Taurus age they had perpetually harassed the Empire ; now they flooded over it and left their traces in France, Spain, Northern Italy, and even Africa. Tacitus says of the Germans that they worshipped Mercury before all other gods, and so this development seems in agreement with our hypothesis.

The Cancer epoch begins about A.D. 540, and, as with

all water-signs, there is a period of intellectual obscuration; we are in fact in the Dark Ages.

They cover the rise of the Papacy—Gregory the Great became pope in 590—and of Muhammedanism—the Hejira was in 622. It is probable that the Roman Catholic Church does, to its members, carry a Cancer significance; that is to say, it is in a very real sense the Mother Church which trains, guides and protects.

As for Muhammedanism, I do not think that can be brought within our scheme except in so far as it impinged upon the western cultures. It is suggested that it probably has its own cycle, possibly dating from the Hejira.

One might expect some great female figures to occur during these times, but this was, of course, something that could not easily occur, taking into account the general level of civilisation. However, one of the most famous monarchs of the time, Justinian, was notoriously wife-ruled. The same emperor has come down to us made famous by the legal codification that took place under his auspices and perhaps that has some connection with the exaltation of Jupiter in Cancer. It is the office of the law to protect the innocent and this protective aspect is quite Cancerian.

The Leo period will be from 720 to 900.

We are still in the Dark Ages, but the coronation of Charlemagne by the Pope, as Holy Roman Emperor, in the year 800 is an event of the first importance and thoroughly in accord with the Leo epoch. Indeed an age of great kings and emperors confronts us, just as, in the time of the Aries predominance, there were the figures of the Cæsars. Under the guidance of these rulers the nations of Europe, arising from the broken remnants of the old empire, take shape. Above all, the French nation begins its career appropriately under a Leo note.

In England, at this time, we have Alfred the Great.

Just as the epoch begins we have the successful defence of Constantinople against the Saracens by Leo the Isaurian. The name may be significant. Constantinople itself is placed under Cancer.

The Virgo epoch begins about 900 and seems only obscurely characterised. One might expect extensive famines and pestilences.

But perhaps one may note the coming into prominence of the Seljuk Turks. Turkey is said to be ruled by Virgo and this may be a racial, not a territorial, rulership.

Another great development was the Magyar surge westward; they completed the conquest of Hungary in 906 and in a few years they had penetrated to the Rhine.

Again, there were the Viking, Norman or Northman invasions and settlements.

I do not know what sign is said to govern the Magyars or the Vikings either, but one would not suppose that there was much affinity with Virgo, except, indeed, that modern Hungary is a great corn-growing country.

The Libra epoch begins about 1080 and is, in my view, very clearly shown indeed. Literature and culture revive, and we come to the age of chivalry and romance.

In 1096 we have the First Crusade. Doubtless most of the crusaders were ruffians, at least by our standards, but it is still true that their expeditions were, at any rate for the best of them, inspired by an ideal.

In 1110 my conspectus mentions one of the first of the miracle plays as being performed, and in 1139 Geoffrey of Monmouth's *History of the Britons*, the basis of all the vast literature of the Arthurian romances, is in existence.

The University of Salerno is said to have been founded in 1150, and the same date is given approximately for the appearance of the Teutonic epic, the *Nibelungenlied*. In 1160 Chrétien de Troyes, one of the great French poets of the period of romance, flourished, and a few years later Oxford University was already established. The University of Paris was founded about 1210.

One must not overlook Arabian scholarship; Averroes died in 1198.

Then there were the troubadours and minnesingers. Walther von der Vogelweide flourished around the beginning of the thirteenth century.

William of Lorris wrote *The Romaunt of the Rose* about 1237, which brings us to the close of the period. Fortunately the cultural seeds sown in the Libra time continue to produce their flowers unto this day, and even in the Scorpio age that follows we have great literary figures, though the work of the greatest of them all, Dante, bears the stamp of the eighth sign clearly enough. The *Inferno* is perhaps the most vindictive work ever penned.

Assuming that Scorpio takes over about 1260, we have the massacre of the Sicilian Vespers in 1282, and before that, in 1252, I see the ominous note that Innocent IV then approved the use of torture for the discovery of heresy.

This period also covers the first use of gunpowder, a compound that has proved the first of so many deadly agencies.

The Hundred Years War between France and England began in 1338 and ended a few years after the epoch of Scorpio. We have also endless Anglo-Scottish conflicts.

Very characteristic was the Black Death, which reached England in 1349 and had immense social consequences.

A higher aspect of the sign is seen in the development in this age of Christian mysticism; one finds such names as Tauler, Ruysbroek, Julian of Norwich.

The Wars of the Roses began in 1455 and thus come into the next period.

It seems that the positive signs always characterise their periods much more clearly than the negative ; and this is indeed only what might be expected.

Sagittarius runs from 1440 to 1620 ; and what a period this is !

The first item in my conspectus is 1440 itself, and under it the entry Invention of Printing with movable types by Coster at Haarlem. It was not till 1475 that the first book was printed in the English language.

In 1453 Constantinople fell to the Turks and as a consequence Greek refugees spread the ancient culture of their race over the west.

The Western Hemisphere was opened by Columbus in 1492 and a long list of dates of eminent geographical discoveries and feats of exploration could easily be compiled, were this necessary. However, these achievements are common knowledge : what must be stressed is that the dominant power, and the one most active in opening up and subduing the New World, is that of Spain—a Sagittarian country.

Moreover, much of the period is known to us as the Elizabethan Age, and it is probable that that monarch was the outstanding figure of the whole age. Her correct ascendant is in Capricorn, but she had Jupiter in Sagittarius.

It would be natural to expect religion to play a great part in a Sagittarian epoch ; and so indeed it does. Martin Luther published his theses at Wittenberg in 1517 and the Reformation rapidly gathered strength. This, again, is common knowledge and there is no need to dwell upon the subject, which nevertheless is as characteristic of the ninth sign as is the spirit of exploration and adventure.

One can even see the Sagittarius signature in the cult of the beard which roughly covers the latter half of this epoch. And at the close, there is the fashion for men to pad their doublets and so enormously exaggerate the parts of the body ruled by Sagittarius. Even in these very transient modes and habits one sees evidence of the truth of Astrology. The Divine Artist has a great love of detail !

One may also see Jupiter at work in the Peasants' Revolt in Germany (1524).

Notice also the founding of the Society of Jesus (1539).

Towards the close we find the beginnings of the religious wars in France.

There are also the beginnings of natural science, in the modern sense. In 1589 Galileo was dropping cannon balls from the leaning tower of Pisa to disprove the Aristotelean doctrine that the speed of falling bodies is determined by their weight. Soon after he was using the telescope—a typically Jovian instrument—and the wonders of the heavens were being revealed in a manner hitherto undreamed of. Copernicus' *De Revolutionibus* had been printed some forty-six years earlier. Kepler began publishing in 1609, towards the end of this epoch.

We come now to Capricorn—1620–1800—the last completed age in modern times. It stands out plainly enough.

As the previous age had been dominated by Spain, so now France assumes a similar rôle. It is also a period of literary classicism, a sharp conflict between profligacy and Puritanism, and an age that saw the founding of modern science.

Is it not more than a coincidence that in this very year 1620 we have Bacon's *Novum Organum* and the sailing of the Pilgrim Fathers for New England ?

There was of course the terrible Thirty Years War in Germany and our own much tamer Civil War. Perhaps one can say that these were political wars, whereas those of earlier periods, such as that of Scorpio, were rather of the nature of pretentious plundering raids. But one often sees the influence of the exaltation-ruler, and Capricorn therefore brings Mars with it.

The Bank of England was founded in 1694.

However, it is unnecessary to specify events when the whole period is well marked with the Capricornian value. The architecture, the very furniture, bears the imprint of the tenth sign. Notice, too, how India comes into the picture.

But the advent of Aquarius is hastened, or at least complicated, by the discovery of Uranus in the year 1781. Already in 1776 there had been the American Declaration of Independence and this was virtually carried into effect by 1781, when Lord Cornwallis surrendered to a Franco-American army at Georgetown.

But the Capricorn ' influence ' lasted well. That very Saturnian work, *The Decline and Fall of the Roman Empire*, was first published in 1776, and so also Adam Smith's *Wealth of Nations*. James Watts patented his steam engine in 1782, and as the epoch ended we come to a veritable revolution, or spate of revolutions, in literature, economic life and politics. Once again, there is no need to particularise, but, as regards literature, it may be observed that Johnson died and Burns' first volume of poems were printed in the same year, 1786.

Louis XVI was executed in 1793. Thomas Paine's *Rights of Man*, a most Aquarian work, had appeared two years earlier.

So we come to the beginning of an Aquarian epoch in 1800. Not *the* Aquarian Age, unless by pure coincidence. That will come, for what it may be worth, when the First Point of Aries enters the constellation Aquarius, which depends upon the true boundary of that constellation.

Of this Aquarian epoch which began in 1800 or thereabouts and will persist until 1980, we know enough without there being any need whatever to examine its trends in detail. Indeed, only specialists in the various fields of human unfoldment could attack such a task without committing an act of unforgivable audacity. An incredible development of natural science has occurred, and there has been a movement towards economic equality and the ideals of humanism, horribly interrupted, it is true, in our own day. This interruption we would like (albeit Aquarius has a cruel side) to ascribe to the entry into the human consciousness of the planet Pluto, the bringer to light of that which lies hidden. When humanity has adjusted itself to that fresh value, the present collapse of international morality may pass away and give place to something more ideal than Europe has previously known.

As to whether the Piscean epoch, to come in 1980, will be ' better ' than the Aquarian, Astrology can but say that it will be *different*. Whether it will be better and more agreeable (which is what most people mean when they say ' better ') depends chiefly upon Man himself. One may venture the assertion that, on the whole, an age ruled by Jupiter and Neptune may be less harsh and less replete with the unexpected than one dominated by Uranus. But the last Piscean epoch, from 180 B.C. to the birth of Jesus, was the time of the decline of the Roman Republic, a time of demoralisation and dissolution. Since then we have travelled a long and painful journey and sometimes one feels that, so far as wisdom goes, we are little the better for our experiences."

Newly Discovered Planets

We have remarked in the above passage on the manner in which the operation of cyclic periods can be complicated by the discovery of fresh planets and have made some remarks on the conditions in the world when Uranus was found in 1781.

Such discoveries always appear to herald revolutions of some sort.

Neptune was found, in typically Neptunian circumstances, in 1846, and 1848 was the " year of revolutions " when the absolutist régime associated with Metternich broke down.

The same period is associated with Chartism, Owen's socialism, and the emancipation of colonial slaves, all in the thirties.

The Ten Hours Act was passed in 1847.

Spiritualism in its modern form began with the alleged phenomena of the Fox Sisters in 1848.

These things have often been pointed out, but they cannot be omitted from a work on political astrology.

As for Pluto, it was followed by all the barbarisms and crudities of Nazism, things that most men had thought of as long outlived but which had only lain hidden, and erupted in Plutonian fashion as the planet came into our consciousness.

It is unnecessary to labour these points, but one must always take into account the possibility of fresh discoveries of a like nature which may upset our forecasts and give human development—one cannot necessarily say progress—a new orientation, as to the nature of which it is only possible to speculate.

CHAPTER SIX

THE SUN, MOON AND PLANETS AND THE SIGNS AND HOUSES IN POLITICAL ASTROLOGY

THE *Sun* stands for the supreme authority in the State, whether this be a monarch or president, royalty and nobility, those in supreme control of whatever department of the national life is under consideration.

Thus eclipses of the Sun tend to affect these. Generally, the Sun, if well-placed, is benefic and benefits whatever house it occupies.

On the other hand, the *Moon* relates to the masses of the people, the Demos, and it has also to do with the Land and crops. It is the significatrix of women, as distinct from men. It is not necessarily beneficial to the matters ruled by the house it occupies, its value depending largely upon sign and aspect.

Mercury rules literature, the Press, education and all who are concerned therewith, the post office and all means of communication. Political speeches and meetings come under this planet and it has also considerable effect upon general trade. It often indicates *changes*.

Like the Moon, its value depends upon sign and aspect.

Venus rules the social and festive side of the national life, society, and Art, and with Mercury it affects literature, especially poetry.

It adds to the national happiness and well-being and tends to preserve peace. But in actual time of war it is a planet of victory.

Mars rules the armed forces and also all trades that minister to these ; it has much to do with engineering.

It has connection with criminality of the violent kind.

It is also related (when coupled with Saturn) to fires.

Associated with Uranus it may cause explosions, both physical and emotional, and has relation with revolutions. With Neptune, it is related to poisonings and treacherous crimes.

It must be watched in connection with epidemic diseases.

Jupiter signifies the clergy and churches, the judges and the law. Banking and insurance are also under this planet, and it tends to affect the " respectable " classes.

It is philanthropic and is associated with movements and institutions of that nature, especially if configured with Neptune.

It points to prosperity and peace.

Saturn stands for landed and house property, and for the formal side of the State, in its ordinative and administrative aspects—the law from the standpoint of its restraining purposes, as distinct from the law that guarantees liberty.

Mines are traditionally placed under this planet, but it is not unlikely that Pluto may to some extent usurp this rulership.

Uranus seems also to have kinship with the administrative officers of the State and their functions. It is not related to the pomp and circumstance of power, which is solar, nor is it, like Saturn, concerned with restrictive legislation, but it represents the administration of power.

Probably it also rules power on the physical plane—dynamos and all power-generators. It is connected with electricity.

In affliction it is rebellious and anarchic.

Neptune is related to Pisces and the 12th house and so pairs with negative Jupiter, having affinity with hospitals and all charitable institutions and organisations, things that exist to help others.

It has relation to the mercantile marine and the Navy.

Under affliction it is connected with confusion, muddle, waste and inefficiency, with treachery and underworld crime and scandal, both sexual and financial.

It is related to brewing and the drink trade, and also perhaps to chemicals, oils, and (possibly) woollens, also footwear.

Likewise it is related to the Theatre and Motion Picture professions, and to Music and other forms of art.

Pluto is connected with mines and all practices that bring the hidden to light.

It is probably active in the Underworld of crime and is a planet of war, quite as much, it seems, as Mars.

Signs and Houses

These may be taken together, for they correspond closely. It may be said, however, that the signs are probably less regarded in mundane astrology than in the natal branch, and that more stress is laid upon the houses.

The *First House* represents the nation as a whole, a unitary political body.

The *Second House* is the economy of the country and its material prosperity ; all that is related thereto, and those closely engaged therewith, from the Chancellor of the Exchequer downwards.

The *Third House*—education, schools and literature of all sorts, especially periodical publications. Post office, radio, telegraphs. All methods of transit, probably including the air lines.

It is said to indicate neighbouring nations and the country's relations with them.

The *Fourth House*—Land and houses, and the produce of the land (though it is suggested that crops probably come under Virgo and the 6th house). The common people.

It is said to represent the Opposition in Parliament.

The *Fifth House* is said to rule all forms of national pleasure and enjoyment, amusements, entertainments, theatres, sports, and all forms of speculation, in their pleasurable aspect rather than when regarded as sources of income.

Children, and the birth-rate, come here, also immorality (when there is affliction) and scandals arising therefrom.

It is said to govern Society and high social functions.

The older astrologers say that ambassadors come under this house, though it is difficult to see why.

The *Sixth House* rules workers and the employed classes generally; the Labour Party.

Public Health.

Green places the armed services and the civil services under this house.

The *Seventh House*—Relations with foreign countries. It is said to be the house of open warfare and enmity, as well as of treaties and alliances; but friendly nations must also be considered under the Eleventh House, and all foreign relations must have some relation with the Ninth.

The collapse of France in 1940 was shown in our national (1801) map by the conjunction of progressed Moon with Saturn in the 11th.

The *Eighth House* rules death and public mortality. Green places here death duties, financial relations with foreign countries, the Privy Council.

The *Ninth House* rules all forms of long-distance travel and communication, such as sea-voyages and all kinds of shipping. All things connected with law and with religion, with philosophy and possibly science, which, however, would probably come largely under the 3rd in its educative and its practical aspects.

The *Tenth House* denotes the rulers, whether monarchs or president, the government in a general sense, and the national prestige and puissance.

It is probably the most important and powerful of all houses in mundane astrology and bodies here have a wide significance. Thus in the vernal ingress figure for 1951 the Festival of Britain does not seem to be in any way indicated by the 5th, as might be expected, but rather by Jupiter, the planet of " the good time," in the 10th.

The *Eleventh House* is said to denote Parliament, especially the House of Commons (Green says it has been proposed that the opposite house, the 5th, denotes the House of Lords, but it is not easy to say why).

He also gives friends of the nation and town and county councils, with which I agree.

The *Twelfth House* will show all philanthropic and reformatory institutions, prisons, hospitals, homes for the afflicted. Underground movements and secret enemies of the State ; secret and occult societies ; monasteries and other forms of institutional religion.

The use of the Houses, whether in political or any other form of Astrology, is at present bedevilled, if one may say so, by the widespread failure of astrologers to agree on the correct method of domification, and as to this each must form his own opinion. A certain amount of evidence could be adduced in favour of more systems than one.

It is certain that prime importance must be given to the Angles, especially when they are in exact aspect with bodies, and to the angular houses.

In equal division the cusps of the 4th and 10th houses do not generally correspond with the meridian line, but this is always of outstanding importance. Similarly, the nonagesimal, or point in precedent square to the ascendant, which is cusp 10 in equal division, must not be neglected; and the "east point," or point where the ecliptic cuts the great circle that passes through the poles of the equator and the east and west points of the horizon,* is also well worth observation.

Students might also advantageously watch the values (if any) of bodies exactly on cusps, as calculated by such methods as those of Placidus, Campanus and Regiomontanus, for it is generally agreed that the cusps are the most effective elements in the houses, and this belief is held by advocates of all systems.

Progressions of planets to cusps may also be studied. For example, Mars (secondary) to cusp 9 in our 1801 map coincided with the Crimean War.

*Easily found by adding 6 hr. to the R.A.M.C. and finding what degree is then on the meridian. Thus if the R.A.M.C. of a map is 1 hr. 18 min., the East Point will be 18 Cancer. Note that this is not the *due* east point of the ecliptic. This falls where the ecliptic cuts the prime vertical, a point that may also repay examination.

APPENDIX ONE

THE calculation of foreign horoscopes will be greatly simplified by the use of the method explained by Mr. G. H. Bailey in *Astrology*, Vol. 24, No. 3.

It may be reduced to the following rules:

1. Adjust birth-time for daylight saving, if any.
2. Turn local standard time, in which the birth has, or should have been, recorded, to the standard time for which your ephemeris is calculated.
3. Calculate sidereal time (R.A.M.C.) for this, in the usual way and making the correction (9.85 sec. per hour) for acceleration of clock-time to sidereal time.*
4. Add to or subtract from this sidereal time the time-difference between the place for which your ephemeris is calculated and the place of birth, at the rate of 4 mins. for each degree.

Take as example the map for the Independence of Burma, January 4, 1948, 4.20 a.m., local standard time, Rangoon.

1. Daylight saving does not apply.
2. Burma time is 6½ hrs. in advance of G.M.T., therefore 4.20 a.m. by the former = 9 h. 50 m. p.m. on Jan. 3, G.M.T.

	hrs.	min.	sec.
3. R.A.M.C. Greenwich Jan. 3 noon =	18	48	07
Add	9	50	00
Acceleration		01	37
	28	39	44
4. Time interval for Rangoon (add for east long.)	6	24	52
	35	04	36
Subtract 24 hrs.	24	00	00
	11	04	36

*The approximate acceleration of 10 sec. per hour is usually employed. If exactitude is required tables are available, or one second may be deducted for every minute. Thus 12 hrs. at 10 sec. an hour equals 2 min., but the precise correction is 1 min. 58¼ sec.

The time interval is obtained by multiplying the difference in longitude by 4 and calling degrees minutes, and minutes seconds.

Thus, Rangoon is 96° 13′ east of Greenwich. Multiplied by 4, this yields 384° 52.′ Calling the degrees minutes and the minutes seconds, we have 6 hrs. 24 min. 52 sec., as above.

This method obviates the 10 sec. per 15° correction entirely, and in obtaining the equivalent G.M.T. time (or whatever time the ephemeris used is based upon) the time for the calculation of planetary positions is also ascertained. In the above example it will be of course for 9 hrs. 50 min. p.m., January 3.

When it is desired to calculate a map for an event, such as an eclipse, the time for which is given in the aspectarian of the ephemeris, it is only necessary to ascertain the sidereal time for the event on the meridian for which the ephemeris is reckoned, and to add or subtract the time-interval between that meridian and the place for which it is desired to erect the map.

Thus the eclipse of September 1, 1951, is stated in Raphael's Ephemeris to have occurred at 0 hrs. 50 min. p.m. Sidereal time at noon at Greenwich on that day was 10 hrs. 39 min. 32 sec., so that the sidereal time on M.C. at the time of the eclipse was, at Greenwich,

hrs.	min.	sec.
10	39	32
	50	00
		08
11	29	40

If we wished to erect a figure for this eclipse at Rangoon we should add 6 hrs. 24 min. 52 sec.

Information as to summer-time regulations and zones of standard time will be found in such works of reference as the *Nautical Almanac* and *Whitaker's*, to which the reader is referred. He will also require a good atlas.

Since the student of political astrology will be in the main concerned with these matters in connection with capital, or at least important, cities, he will not be confronted with the difficulties that meet those who have to erect figures for remote districts where, at least in some countries, the rural population disregarded summer-time during the war and possibly still do so.

In cases of difficulty the appropriate official of the local Embassy or Legation will usually furnish data.

APPENDIX TWO

List of Cities with Suggested Astrological Affinities

THESE are based on Coley's work published in 1676, to which a few modern examples have been added. Nearly all these attributions must be regarded as tentative in the extreme.

Aries — Naples, Capua, Ancona, Florence (name suggests ♀), Verona, Utrecht, Padua, Cracow.
Modern ascriptions: Birmingham, Leicester, possibly most of the west Midlands.

Taurus — Mantua, Tarentum, Lucerne, Leipzig.
Perhaps Dublin. Eastbourne, Hastings and much of Sussex.

Gemini — London, Metz, Bruges, Nuremburg.
Modern ascriptions: Melbourne, Plymouth, Cardiff.

Cancer — Amsterdam, Constantinople, Milan, Venice, York, St. Andrew's.
Modern: New York, Manchester and probably much of Lancashire.

Leo — Rome, Prague, Syracuse, Damascus.
Modern: Portsmouth, Bath, Bristol, Chicago, Philadelphia, Los Angeles.

Virgo — Paris, Lyons, Heidelberg, Jerusalem, Corinth, Athens.
Modern: Boston (U.S.A.), Reading. Most towns connected with the fruit-growing industry or seed-marketing, and most spas and health-resorts, probably have a strong Virgo element.

Libra Vienna, Antwerp, Lisbon, Freiburg, Copen hagen, Frankfort-on-Main.

In modern times Leeds and Nottingham hav been placed under Libra.

Scorpio By tradition, Fez in Morocco, and Valenci The ancients appear to have hesitated t ascribe the sign they so much disliked to an prominent cities, but moderns have not show this delicacy. Green, in his useful manua gives amongst others Dover, Halifax, Hul Liverpool, Newcastle, Stockport and Worthin It seems probable that much of the north-ea of England is under Scorpio. Green also give Washington, New Orleans, Milwaukee, S John's (Newfoundland).

Sagittarius Toledo (Spain, and also Ohio ?), Stuttgar Budapest, Cologne.

Modern attributions : Nottingham (also place by Green under Libra), Bradford and Sheffiel It is quite likely that Yorkshire, with its famou sporting traditions, is under this sign.

Capricorn Coley gives Oxford and Ghent.

It is quite likely that Delhi and Mexico Cit come under this sign. The administrative par of most cities, as Westminster and Whitehall.

Aquarius Hamburg, Bremen, Salzburg and Trent occu in Coley.

Green puts Salisbury under both this and th preceding sign. Brighton is probably a tru ascription. Very likely Stockholm and Lenin grad and/or Moscow.

Pisces Coley gives a few famous cities—Alexandri Seville, Worms, Ratisbon, Campostella.

Green gives a fairly large list in Great Britai Bournemouth and the neighbourhood a almost certainly under Pisces.

It will be seen that even these hypothetical allocations are very few in number and a wide field lies open for investigation. Coats of arms, careful observation of conditions prevailing at the times of important civic events or natural catastrophes (such as fires), nativities of persons prominent in the civic life, important industries (e.g., fishing or shoe-making = Pisces, hat-making, as at Luton, = Aries), dates of charters : all these may provide clues which, taken together, may give something approaching practical certainty.

It is a branch of Astrology which might most profitably be developed, especially from the standpoint of the individual. For it cannot be questioned that it is wise and well to inhabit, if possible, a district ruled by a planet which is strong in one's nativity, and on the other hand to avoid those which have hostile rulers.

APPENDIX THREE

List of Countries with Suggested Astrological Affinities

THESE are also based upon Coley's work, with some suggested modern attributions. Upon the whole the rulerships of countries are probably more reliable than those of cities. These should be regarded as natural affinities, distinct from the rulerships of particular dynasties, forms of government, and other political factors.

Aries	England, France, Germany, Upper Silesia, Poland, Burgundy, Denmark, Syria, Palestine.
Taurus	Russia, Greater Poland, Sweden, Lorraine, Campania, Switzerland, Rhaetia, Franconia, Parthia, Persia, Cyclades, Ireland. Russia is placed nowadays under Aquarius, and so also, I think, Sweden. The habits of the ancient Parthians suggest Sagittarius.
Gemini	Sardinia, Lombardy, West of England and Wales, Flanders, Armenia, Lower Egypt, Belgium, the U.S.A. (but some American astrologers favour Saturn rising in Libra as their national *political* map).
Cancer	Scotland, Holland, Burgundy, Numidia and Africa and the African races generally, Bithynia, according to some, Germany. Green adds Paraguay. China (or Libra).
Leo	France, Italy, the Alps, Rumania, Bohemia, Sicily, Chaldea and Phœnicia.
Virgo	Greece, Crete, Croatia, Mesopotamia, Babylonia, Assyria, part of France, Lower Silesia, Virginia, Brazil, Turkey, Switzerland, West Indies.

A similar division in latitude from the north pole would put om 60° north to 30° under Taurus, so that Great Britain ould be divided in longitude between Aries (east) and Pisces vest) and in latitude would fall under Taurus. So also, for nat matter, would France and Spain.

It is clear that such a system and any others like it could only e valid, if at all, from one point of view and would have to be ipplemented from other angles. The meridian of Greenwich an artificial, not a natural, conception and a division of the urface of the globe founded upon it could only have such value the human mind could give it.